The ABC's of Widowhood

Pat Nowak

ISBN: 1-4107-4726-3 (e-book)
ISBN: 1-4107-4725-5 (Paperback)

Library of Congress Control Number: 2003093914

This book is printed on acid free paper.

Printed in the United States of America
Bloomington, IN

1stBooks – rev. 07/09/03

Acknowledgements

To my children Martin and Laura, who have been sources of laughter, comfort and joy? Without them, life would have been unbearable. To my son in law Doug and my daughter in-law Heather, thank you for being there for us through thick and thin. To my grandchildren Liam and Rae and those to come, I will always try to see life through your eyes, because that is truly what life is about.

To my family and friends...thank you for being the continuous emotional aid I needed. To Dean Harris for his creative cover and book artistry and to Rich Iott, who deserves a medal for making something out of my somewhat neglected notes, you both truly are priceless jewels.

To Dr. Lou Tartaglia for believing in my quest, for Cy Dunlap, Marina Lung and Vic Steinbach who gave their thoughtful comments and Ron Welty and Norm Koenigsecker for helping me with editing and computer skills. To Tom Specht who was a kind buffer for the anxiety and trepidation I felt, and to Jean Smith, Linda Kosinski and Joan Kelly, all widows, who relived their grief and gave me insightful comments on the book.

And finally to my late husband, Casimir...we did not have an opportunity to say goodbye, but please know that everything I am, I owe to your belief that I could do anything I set my mind to.... thank you.

Finally, for every woman who has lost a partner...just believe in tomorrow, for it will get better if you let it.

TABLE OF CONTENTS

Reviews

The ABC's of Widowhood is filled with precious pearls of wisdom. Its greatest value is the healing it brings to the fragile soul of the broken hearted. Every widow needs and deserves this treasure.

Louis A. Tartaglia, MD Author, The Great Wing, a parable

"Until death do us part"... but no bride and groom thinks this will really happen to her or him. Not today, not tomorrow, not ever. The denial of death is a psychological defense without which daily life would be unbearable. Even after the death of a loved one, in the beginning, the feeling of shock and denial is there to protect us from the deepest emotional pain of living, GRIEF.

In over 25 years of practice, grief-counseling cases are by far the most difficult for me and I suspect for most professionals. First of all, our own fear surfaces and our wall of denial thins in the process. Sometimes we even struggle to find those words of comfort but we find them. Comfort and the ultimate acceptance of the death of a husband come through a foundation of multiple resources. I often recommend books and support groups for women as an adjunct to individual counseling. The therapeutic benefits of shared experiences and role models for survival are very powerful for healing.

In The ABC's of Widowhood, Pat Nowak is the role model women need. She provides an exceptional description of the stages of grief along with supporting secrets for adjustment to the trauma of the death of a husband. A trauma, no woman believes she can survive, let alone fully live again. This book is a definite survival guide for dealing with oneself, children, family, friends and finances. These are critical areas, which she provides both practicality and wisdom.

Marina B. Lung, M.A. Clinical Psychologist

The ABC's of Widowhood is a comprehensive yet user-friendly guide to coping with the death of a life long companion. As a therapist who has worked with many clients suffering from the trauma of losing a loved one, I found the information straightforward, yet, presented in a very sensitive, caring manner. Often confusion, uncertainty, and a feeling of being totally overwhelmed compound the grieving process. Ms. Nowak's book will help the reader unravel the mysteries, which will be facing them now and in the future. I strongly recommend this book to any woman coping with the loss of her spouse through death or even divorce.

Vic Steinbach, MSW, CSW

Ms. Nowak has written the most helpful guide for surviving widowhood, I have ever read. The ABC's of Widowhood is simply done, yet filled with extremely meaningful information and the book makes one of life's most difficult experiences easier to cope with. Practical and to the point, this is the guidebook to put on your nightstand to pick up when you are in need of some helpful hints to face life. As a counselor, it is difficult to find such supportive information to put into the hands of grief stricken women, yet Ms. Nowak's easy format will be a benefit over and over as a woman moves through the grieving process. My appreciation to Ms. Nowak for this gift.

Cy Dunlap, L.C.E.S.C. Guidance Counselor

Pat and I have been friends for many years and now we are widows together. Her strength and wisdom have encouraged me through two years in widowhood. I am truly proud of her accomplishment with this book. It gives a clear and concise account of the feelings and attitudes of being a widow, plus sound advice on financial and legal matters. You see yourself in many of the references. The book helped me understand why I felt the way I did and made me realize I am not alone.

Linda Kosinski

I read this book twice and marveled at what a wonderful and educational learning experience it was. This book is a reference for what you need in all aspects of your life for the future…alone. I only wish I had read it sooner, so much more would have been easier for me to understand.

Jean Smith

I cannot tell you how encouraging it was to read your book. It has been six months and it was comforting to know many of the feelings I am experiencing are normal; I was reassured that I am not alone. Through your words I know these feelings will pass and life does go on in a positive manner. I wish there were a way to get this information into the hands of a woman before they are faced with this tragic situation. They need to hear positive, good solid advice when a death occurs and the knowledge that they will make it through these difficult circumstances. By knowing what you will be up against and being prepared can help immensely. This manual, very delicately, brings up topics that need to be discussed and suggests results that will have a positive outcome.

I also found the format easy to read and I will continue to use it in the future, as a quick reference, when a situation occurs and I need a quick pick-me-up or a fast piece of good advice. I would recommend this resource a required reading for everyone. My sister, a non-widow also enjoyed the book and I am honored that you shared this manuscript with us.

Joan Kelly

FOREWARD

I hired Pat Nowak. That was seventeen years ago. First as a public relations consultant and then, after a year, as the public relations and consumer affairs director of the company of which I was president and chief executive officer. This was no small potatoes. It was a terrific regional supermarket chain, which dominated nearly all of its markets and did nearly three-quarters of a billion dollars in business annually. She was the consummate public relations professional: sharp, witty, pushy, and aggressive. She knew how to make it in the world and how to shape public opinion. She knew how to make people like her (or at least appreciate her) even as she stepped on their toes to get done what she needed done for the company. Our company had what could only be called a positive relationship with the press. Our community image among consumers - our competitor's as well as our own - set records in the industry. We were so foremost in the minds of consumers that consumer studies showed we even received credit for community events our competitors sponsored! It was all Pat's doing.

But she was a horrific writer. She wrote like she talked: in machine-gun bursts of enthusiasm which truly demanded, "you had to be there" to understand. So I became her editor out of immediate necessity.

I knew her husband. I knew him as a quiet and unobtrusive man who, honestly, seemed like a peculiar match for Pat. He was an employed in the auto industry while she, by necessity, traveled the society circle. But while they were light-years apart on the surface, it was clear that somewhere in their souls they were deeply connected. They had two truly wonderful children.

Over the years, Pat and I have been professionally very close. Our instincts and thoughts worked well together. We were household names and faces throughout the region for nearly ten years based on our hundreds of down-home (and sometimes goofy) television commercials. We co-hosted the number one Saturday morning radio show in the market for eight years. I thought I knew her pretty well.

I wasn't there when Pat learned of her husband's death, but I admired how she handled it all. I was there eighteen days later when she learned that her house - and all her possessions save the clothes on her back - had burned to the ground. In fact, I was the one who got the call and told her. That was on Saturday night. She took the day off Monday and was back to work on Tuesday. It seemed to me to be a typical Nowak-superwoman-rebound.

When she asked me to edit this book I was flattered. But I also assumed it would be like the hundreds of other Pat Nowak things I had edited in the past. I was quite wrong. Not only had she learned to write (or maybe I never noticed it before?) but also I discovered a Pat Nowak I had never known. I discovered a woman who was scared, resentful, lacking in self-confidence, and who felt alone in the world. Never in a thousand years would I have guessed it. I knew a consummate professional who never let her own private tribulations affect her professional life. I discovered a person as delicate as a child but as strong as an iron rod.

I also came to realize that this book, while styled as a self-help guide for women in her unfortunate circumstance, was also part of the healing and the closing of a difficult chapter in her life. It was part inspiration and part therapy. And in that I found a special message: that one must close that chapter in some way and go on. It can be as complex as writing a book or as simple as looking at yourself in the mirror. But there must be closure.

I also realized that what we see on the surface is not always true. The strong can be weak and the weak can be pillars of strength in times of stress. Never limit the strength of your future by focusing on your weaknesses of today. Deep inside, we all have tremendous resources of strength. The trick is to dig deep enough, without giving up, to find them.

Enjoy this book as I did. Don't read it cover to cover... pick it up and browse it from time to time. Many of the thoughts you will find in here are important gems of knowledge for anytime in your life; not just for when you have crossed the threshold of widowhood. If you are reading this because of an impending death, take counsel of its advice to prepare. If you are reading this after the fact, take its advice to heart. Do not despair. There is indeed, life after death on *both* *sides* of the River Jordan.

Rich Iott, Braeburn Croft Farm

The ABC's of Widowhood

I wish there had been a primer written for widows. There are books for children entering school, for your high school years, college manuals, and self-help novels for new moms, old moms, menopause, and everything else under the sun. But I have read nothing that tells you what to expect when a part of your life ends.

When a spouse dies, through a process of trial and error, most women tread the tightrope of life not fully understanding all that is going on around them. And there is really no one who can get to the depths of the pain, anger and fright. Your days are spent walking alone through a haze, not fully comprehending what you should do next and yet you must go forward. There are arrangements to be made, family to cope with, and countless other duties that come with the new title "WIDOW".

My widowhood came suddenly. My husband had been sick for five years with a non-threatening illness made worse by an alcohol addiction. After overcoming the dependence, our lives were sailing along smoothly. Since both children were away at school, our routine was fairly normal. We had come to mutually respect each other's space and were great friends. However, one day at 7:20 AM, I received a call telling me my husband had been killed. He had been crossing the street when an uninsured motorist, in a hurry, ran into him and he died instantly. I remember screaming but nothing else. I know that someone took me to the hospital that I did call my daughter at school, and I enlisted her fiancée to go to my son's apartment to talk to him, as there was no answer to my phone call.

I was definitely making decisions in an out-of-body state. It was like I was in a dream world and was just waiting to wake up. I chose the funeral home because it was close to home, not from any personal experience. I was lucky, as they were wonderful. I selected the casket by its name, Titan. My son's high school football team was called the Titans. My floral pieces were personal favorites and the clothes he wore were items he had just received for his 51st birthday.

However, because his family was also involved, I became overly sensitive to making everyone feel comfortable with my decisions.

The one thing I remember most vividly is waking up early the morning after his death and sitting in my family room. It was February and in the Midwest, it was cold. I made myself a cup of coffee and stared out at the stars. One shot across the sky and I remember tears coming to my eyes and thinking, "What am I going to do now? How will I get through this?" I had two children in college and knew something about finances. But I was not prepared for making my life's decisions knowing that my future was riding on those decisions.

Since my husband's death was an accident, it suddenly became news and reporters, began pestering me, asking for any tidbit of information. I gave them none. This was a personal moment, not one to be played over and over on the six o'clock news. The days preceding the funeral were another matter. As the PR director for a large regional supermarket chain, I came in contact with hundreds of people on a regular basis and many were kind enough to show up at the viewing. However, I was not prepared for the 236 floral baskets and 1500 people that stood in line to speak to me. The minutes melted into hours and I could not tell you, from one minute to the next, who was there and who was not

I selected my husband's boyhood church for his funeral services and since we were not members, I only spoke briefly to the priest. I was amazed and gratified how eloquently he spoke about someone he had personally never met. Our daughter recited a beautiful poem, one that she had brought back from college, filled with haunting words to a song by a local group. I am sure my husband would have approved.

I like to think that my family and I were strong. We all survived the funeral. I sent my daughter back to school, my son back to his apartment, and I went back to work trying to get my new life started. However, that was not quite to be. Before I could get into the tasks of being a widow, I was presented another challenge. On a Saturday evening, eighteen days after the death of my husband, our house burned the result of a refrigerator fire. My daughter, who had come into town for the weekend, and I were attending a birthday party at the time and were summoned to come home from the party. We found the burned out shell that had been home for nineteen years. As I stood with the firefighters looking at the smoldering ashes, I realized

I truly had nothing left but my children. Even our pet dog perished in the fire.

Today, looking back, my children and I like to think that the fire was somehow the work of my husband. I have read several books and many say when someone dies suddenly they are given a short time on earth, as a spirit, to tie up any loose ends.

Our house was on two acres, a larger house than I needed, and certainly time consuming with all the yard work. There were two two-car garages and a basement workshop full of machinery, tools and his collectibles. I really didn't know where to start. When my husband died, I was aware that keeping the house would be foolish for one person. However, this was the only home our children had ever known and I did not want to add more upheaval or anguish to their lives. They were already in enough pain. But the fire truly gave us a new beginning.

My family and several friends came back early Sunday morning to help pick up any pieces of our lives we could find in the rubble. The amazing things we found intact made us wonder. The house had burned nearly to the foundation, but there were a few odd spots that survived. Incredibly, our boxes of pictures, that chronicled our life, were smoke filled but fine. The jewelry my husband had purchased for me was found safe and sound. Most amazing was that in the rubble of the family room, we found intact and unharmed, the movies and videos we had taken through the years. There was nothing else salvageable but we had all we needed to go on with our lives...our history and ourselves.

I have learned so much since his death eight years ago, some good, some bad. The idea for this book came about during this time as I dealt with attorneys, insurance adjusters, new relationships, old relationships, children, grandchildren, car accidents, employee downsizing, and more. I thought seriously about what women go through when a spouse dies and how little help they actually receive. This is why I wrote The ABC's of Widowhood. We are all familiar with a dictionary and how we can open the page to a word and learn distinctly what it means. That is what this book is for...open to a page and find the word you need to add more clarity to your life. You can use this book now and later. Many of the words will comfort and soothe, but I believe many will make you think. With this in mind I pray you find some peace in your new life.

Pat Nowak

A

Abandoned - The first word you think about at death is that someone has abandoned you. That sense of being abandoned does not go away easily. Whenever something goes wrong in your life that old feeling will creep up on you. At this time it is necessary to busy yourself with other things. Call a friend; go out to dinner. The feeling will soon pass.

Absent-minded - As a new widow you will find yourself quite absent-minded. You will begin to doubt your sanity as you forget simple appointments and day-to-day happenings. This is normal and your forgetfulness will subside. Your mind is overloaded with so much that mundane tasks seem to fall by the wayside. For the time being, place a big calendar near your phone. As an appointment or task comes up list it on your calendar. Make sure that every morning upon waking, you check your calendar, at least until your mind clears.

Accident - Widows can be prone to accidents because their minds wander. I was in a serious car accident five months after my husband died. It was my fault because my mind was not on my driving. It is very important that you take your time when driving or doing household tasks. Don't hurry; take your time with things that need to be done. And if it is possible, hire some outside help for your major chores. That would be a plus.

Action - There will be many times when you will need to take decisive action. You must gather all your strength from deep within and make decisions. It will be hard at first especially if your husband was responsible for your financial well-being. Make sure you do your research and then act accordingly. You will make some wrong decisions. Simply regroup and correct them. Remember that a good decision made today is often better than the perfect decision made tomorrow.

Administrator - As administrator of the estate, you will be expected to be knowledgeable about what is necessary to settle the estate. When seeking basic information, check with the research desk of your local library, university or law school. Many television and radio stations have an "ask an attorney" program and the local bar association may also have some basic information or can refer you to qualified estate attorneys. Unless you are an attorney, you will need to seek professional advice. Since all state laws differ, be sure to talk to someone in your state. One note of caution: be careful of financial or other personal details you share in seeking information. DO NOT provide details to strangers no matter how helpful they seem.

Advice - It is often difficult to ask for advice. I know when I first became a widow I did not want to bother people with small, petty concerns that I had. Several times things went awry because I acted without thinking or discussing the problem with a professional. Jot down questions as they come up and then call someone who can give you an answer. Note the name of the person, the time and date of the reply along with the response. It is easier to review written information than to try to remember it. If the information you receive doesn't seem complete enough, seek more information before you act on it.

Afresh - Your life must start afresh. It will be difficult to think of one instead of two. For several months you will refer to things in a dual role ("we" and "us" instead of "I" and "me"). This is temporary. You must start to think of your life singly instead of together. For many women this will be difficult - especially if you and your husband had a particularly close relationship. Start by exploring activities you have always wanted to do but had no time because of your family duties. Add more as you feel comfortable.

Afterlife - I believe there is an afterlife. I did not come by these thoughts easily. I was not prone to hocus pocus or magical beings. But I believe there is someone who watches over a widow. Several times when I needed a boost because I was feeling blue something quite mysterious would always happen to help me out. If it had occurred only one time I would have thought nothing about it, but it has happened several times throughout the years. My advice...just let it happen!

Alcohol - Be careful! As a new widow it will be very easy to drown your sorrows in a bottle, even if you were never inclined to do so before. But that will only add to your problems. Watch yourself carefully at this time and if you feel like you are overindulging, talk to a mental health therapist or a friend you can trust. Don't try to deal with it alone. The shame lies not in asking for help, but in *not* asking.

Alone - No matter how old or young you are when a spouse dies, you truly feel alone. No matter how many family or friends you have, they cannot and will not take the place of your spouse. The little things that you took for granted will suddenly bring you to tears. It happened to me two weeks after my husband's death. It was Valentine's Day and his ritual was to buy me flowers for every special occasion. In the afternoon, it finally dawned on me that I would not be getting flowers and I could not hold back the tears. The loneliness I felt on that day repeated itself many, many times after that. What I did when I felt desolate was to get out of the house. I would get in my car and go shopping, to the library, or visit a friend. Usually a change of scenery will be just the thing to kick the "lonesome blues" away.

Allocate - It will be necessary to learn to allocate your time, money and resources. If your husband was the financial whiz, it will be necessary to learn or relearn basic finances; if he was the gatekeeper for vacations, household projects etc., you will have to step in and take on some of the tasks. You will be uneasy doing this at first but through trial and error; you will gain new confidence and soon will feel pretty proud of your accomplishments. My first independent achievement was fixing the lights at my new condo. When they all came on the first evening I smiled quite brightly...you can too. An important caveat to this is to make sure before tackling tasks, that may present hazards or require special tools, to ask for help..."when in doubt, ask first". In the early stages, please make sure you allocate enough time for yourself.

Angels - Don't let anybody kid you, there *are* angels. You may never see them. You may never touch or smell them...but they are there. I don't know how many times I have had uneasy moments that suddenly and unexplainably cleared up. As a new widow, angels help you through the rough spots. My advice is to name your angel (mine's Annie) and allow yourself to accept their help and guidance...they will always be around. Thank goodness!

There is someone watching over you...........don't be afraid
to ask a higher power for help

Anger - As a widow, it is easy to be angry. Everything you have known and been comfortable with has been taken away and you feel angry. It's good for you to express these feelings and it is part of the healing process. But, beware, anger can also be destructive. It can turn inward and make you bitter and resentful. You cannot heal until you open your heart and mind and let the rage out. It will take time...it will not happen overnight. Grief therapists encourage you to talk about your anger; this may be only to a friend. By expressing your feelings, the resentment will begin to subside, eventually allowing you to return to a more normal you.

Anniversary - This word will never mean the same as it had previously. You will still celebrate birthdays and special occasions, but "anniversary" will come to mean another year has gone by since your spouse has passed. The anniversary month will find you anxious and reliving the sad memories all over again. Don't panic. Make sure you keep busy. My husband died on the last day in January and his birthday was also in January. Every January without fail my heart goes cold. I make sure that month I am extra busy so I don't wallow in self-pity. I can also say with some conviction that your life gets easier after the first full year of living through each holiday without your spouse.

Annuity - This is a means of investing for your future. Your funds come back in periodic annuity payments when you retire. Speak to an investment counselor, if this is something you may want to pursue.

Apology - Widowhood often finds you being curt, almost rude at times to people who have no idea what has happened in your life. The clerk at the store, someone on the phone, a neighbor, or your children will all incur your wrath from time to time. Apologize as quickly as you can. If not, you will feel even worse. But better yet before the words are spoken, think what effect they will have. Perhaps, that will allow you a moment to think before overreacting.

Assert - The one thing a new widow must learn to do is to assert herself. You may be lied to, treated unfairly, made to feel downright stupid and sometimes harassed by any number of ignorant souls. This is the time to speak up. After the death and fire, I knew I was not going to rebuild on the old lot. Yet I allowed myself to be harassed by a builder hired by the insurance company who insisted that I must rebuild. Instead of reporting this man to the insurance company, I fretted and made myself sick. When I finally got the courage to speak up, the issue was resolved quickly. DO NOT ALLOW ANYONE TO TAKE ADVANTAGE OF YOU. No one can, unless you give him or her permission to by not speaking up for your rights.

Attitude - This very important word will make a BIG difference in your life. How you react to the death will set the tone for the rest of your life. Are you going to be a victim forever? Many women are. I have met several widows who absolutely astonish me with their self-pity and unwillingness to start a new life. No one plans on facing death but a positive attitude can do wonders to help put you back on your feet. A positive attitude needs to begin immediately upon death. There must be no chips on the shoulder, no "oh me...poor me". Believe me; a woman who greets each day with a resolve to face whatever comes her way will soon have more happier moments than sad ones. It is all a matter of attitude.

Attorney - After a death there is much to be done. Estate taxes, wills to probate, insurance matters, so many things and so little you will know or understand. It is best to seek legal advice through your family attorney, a trusted family member or friend. Your own attorney can walk you through the process. If you are unable to hire an attorney, most cities have a legal aid society, with attorneys, who work pro-bono (without a fee) or for a nominal fee. Also, many radio and television stations have call in shows or visit the library as they have reference books that can help you find some answers. For your peace of mind and protection, it is best to consult an attorney.

Autopsy - This procedure is performed when someone dies suddenly of unknown causes or an accident. Usually this procedure takes a day and then the body is released to the funeral home. If your husband had a known illness, it is usually not necessary to perform an autopsy. Local laws will probably make this decision for you.

Awkward - Widowhood makes a woman feel awkward. You are always the fifth wheel. Your friends will be kind, at first, but you present a problem. The world is made for twosomes. You are one. I consider myself lucky; not one of my friends deserted me. Not one wife looked at me like I was going to run away with her husband.

10

Unfortunately, all women are not as lucky as I am. Many times, a new widow is shunned at just the time that she needs to be embraced. If and when you feel as if you are not welcome, it is time to find new friends. Make plans to attend a church group for widows and widowers. Ask to be included in events that single people will be attending at work. Volunteer at charity and school events, for it is there that you will have the opportunity to meet other single, widowed, and divorced men and women. Please remember...there is nothing wrong with you, personally. If a friend should drop you, it is their ignorance. Put on your best smile and find another opportunity...even if it means going alone.

B

Backward - As a widow your life may take a backward step. If you have few assets you may find yourself with another set of problems. You may be forced to downsize, find a job, make do with less and formulate tough decisions at the most difficult time of your life. What can you do? You can sit yourself down with a paper and pencil and take stock of your situation. Be honest! You alone will be able to evaluate your assets, your lifestyle and decide what must be done. By taking this direct action yourself, you will slowly become confident of the steps you must take, in order of their priority: critical first, moderate and long term. Don't be afraid to ask for help when you need advice or are not sure of the steps that you must take. By taking control...you can minimize the backward slide to baby steps and come out ahead.

Bailout - It may be necessary to make some. difficult financial decisions and you may need someone to help bail you out financially, for a short period of time, until insurance becomes available. Be up front and honest. If you need help from a family member or friend, ask. Don't be afraid to talk with your banker or an employer. Understand and discuss your financial position honestly with only those who you feel can help you make the correct decisions and make them aware that your needs will be temporary. Longer-term help, if necessary, can be addressed when you have a better handle on your needs.

Balance - Slowly you need to feel your way to find "balance" in your life. There are several things that will need your personal focus. Your bank balance will have to meet your financial needs but you will also have to find some personal balance in your life. Since your world has been turned upside down you need to explore ways to get your life to a normal state. Stability will be different for everyone. Some women will need time and space to heal; others will need friends and activities to make the transition. One note of caution is to take things slow...if something feels uncomfortable, leave it for another day. The first time I went out to a bar with divorced friends, I left after ten minutes because I did not feel comfortable. Balance takes time and patience...you will find it in time and when you do you are on the path to recovery. Writing in a journal is helpful. You can reread your entries and watch the progress being made...seeing the positive changes helps you be aware that you are finding your balance.

Bank - This is the place that houses your financial destiny. Do you have checking and savings accounts? Make sure you know with whom you bank and how to get your money out. If you are faced with a lengthy illness prior to death, make plans to transfer funds to live comfortably. If you are faced with an immediate death, your first stop should be the bank where you take out enough money to last at least two months.

Bankruptcy - At times bankruptcy is necessary. If you have more debts than assets, it is time to speak to a credit counselor. Some things to remember: gather all of your financial data and determine your assets and liabilities. Review what types of compensation will be coming in from insurance, social security, money from your spouse's previous employer, checking and savings accounts, stock portfolios and 401K's. All of these will be your assets. Now look at your debt column. Hopefully, you will have enough assets to outweigh the debt liability and be able to save something for your future. A point to consider: is that your husband's estate can file for bankruptcy, which does not affect you. This literally wipes away any debt that was in his name only. You should notify these creditors that he is deceased and that you are unable to pay the debt. You may receive one or two threatening letters; however, this is usually all that they can do.

Barricade - It is so easy as a new widow to put a barricade around yourself and your heart. In many cases it is simplest to sit home, not being accessible to family, friends or acquaintances. We allow ourselves to wallow in self-pity because we can't get hurt if we don't feel. If after two months you still are not ready to pursue activities and take phone calls, it might be time to consult a mental health professional. With the fire in my past I got so wrapped up in dealing with the fire details that the death was pushed out of my mind. When I was stricken with some health problems and a bit of depression, months later, I learned that I had Delayed Stress Syndrome. It is easier to deal with stress when you meet it head on.

Beautify - What can a woman do to help herself through a trying time... one thing I highly recommend is to do something for you. Get a new hairstyle, shop for some clothes, go on an exercise program, or beautify your surroundings... plant a garden, paint a room. When you undertake something that adds beauty to your life it has a way of uplifting your spirit like nothing else I know. And remember, beauty does not have to be expensive... it can be the process that makes the difference.

Belief - Whenever death comes calling, you question your belief in a loving God, and in mankind. You tend to go through a period where the anger you feel makes you take time out from God...that is not unusual. You will in time come to understand that death is not necessarily an end to your life. Through prayer and consultation with your religious advisor, you will find some peace of mind, freeing you to again continue your communication with family and loved ones.

Beneficiary - This term is used to identify any funds from insurance policies or other accounts owned by your husband where you were listed as the beneficiary. Generally insurance funds are not a part of probate, therefore, not taxed. It is imperative that you change your will and insurance policies as soon as possible, making sure that your personal wishes for the future are complied with.

Benefits - Often you have certain benefits through your husband's former employer. This may include a 401K, health and life insurance, dental and vision benefits. It is up to you to sit down with the Human Resources department to find out which benefits may continue and which will be terminated. This will allow you time to make arrangements for other alternatives (especially when it comes to health insurance).

Bills - The shock of new responsibilities often sends a new widow screaming. If you were not the financial guru in your family, you will be shortly. Your public library is a great place to seek information. There are all sorts of reference books and articles, etc. that will help you get on the right financial track. It is important that you put your newfound responsibility, as chief financial officer, to work by putting together a budget for your future and your plans to maintain your financial well-being. Once made, stick to those plans. It can be tempting to spend your way to feeling better. You will learn some decisions about money will be tough, but necessary for your survival.

Bittersweet - You will have many bittersweet memories. Often you will remember your spouse fondly and then at other times you will curse under your breath and get angry that he left you all alone. Now it is up to you alone to face events that should have had a family presence. I remember when my daughter got married a year and a half after the death; I was still so consumed with conflicting feelings that it was difficult at times to get through the day. Take a deep breath; remember the good and bad... and know it is understandable to shed a tear. Even to this day, I have hard times occasionally. I have gone through two weddings, a family death, and new grandchildren on my own. Do not let your sadness spoil the occasion for others. Years after the death each occasion will still be bittersweet in some way.

Black - The past consensus has been that upon death the widow, children and house are swathed in black and mourning takes place for one year. Your spouse would probably not be happy about this... I am sure that he would want you to celebrate his life and to do so is an honor to his legacy. You don't need black to do this. Choose the colors he loved in life and use them in his funeral, flowers and in dress. I chose bright funeral flowers, wore a dress I knew he loved and chose his most comfortable clothes for the showing. Words of advice... don't think you have to put your spouse in clothing he hated to wear during life. My husband hated suits and I chose a favorite sweater and shirt for this trip through eternity.

Blend - How does one blend two new lifestyles and become a balanced individual? It is not easy, but if you take some time to evaluate the changes in your life you can come up with some concrete solutions that will take the best aspects of your married life and blend them into your single life. We always enjoyed family vacations and I believed that the death would severely impact that time. However, our first Christmas after the death we started a new tradition. My children and I spent Christmas in Barbados, someplace we had never visited, and we had a great time... it strengthened our family relationship. To this day we try to steal family vacations, when possible, and have blended our old traditions with new ones.

Bombard - You will be bombarded with advice and help from anyone who walks and talks! Everyone will have an opinion about what it will take to get you back on your feet. Smile, listen and discard any information that you don't want or need. If a person persists, thank them for their concern but be emphatic about needing to find your own way. You can benefit by learning tactful communication skills early on.

Books - There are many books that will help you through this difficult period. I chose books that helped me understand the death process. But you will also need financial books, self-help books, and just plain, old lose-yourself-in-great-fiction books. Books will help you get through the endless hours you used to spend with your spouse. If you don't have one, sign up for a library card; there is a wealth of information waiting for you there.

Brave - It will take all of your courage to be brave... brave at the pre showing, meeting friends and callers, brave at the funeral and memorial services, and brave in the days after. Being brave, however, does not mean to suppress your feelings or become so passive that you seem unfeeling. It does mean, taking a stand when needed, expressing your wants, and sticking to your ideals.

Breakdown - During the first year you will find yourself breaking out in tears at the most awkward times. Something little will pierce your heart and the next thing you know the waterworks will start. This is normal; you are going through a process and it will take time for you to shore up your resolve. Until that time, excuse yourself, shed that tear and get back to what you were doing. I want you to know that to this day, there are certain times and events that the tears still come, even eight years later.

Pat Nowak

C

Camera - The pictures that came from your camera probably tell the story of your life. Do not put pictures away and pretend your former life did not happen. Many women do not want to look at pictures because they trigger the hurt. By bringing up the hurt, you are also remembering all the positive things that happened in your life. Pictures chronicle that life...eighteen days after my husband died, our house burned down. Our pictures were miraculously saved and that is the history we used to start our new life. Now I use my camera regularly to continue our family legacy...so should you.

Capacity - We all have a certain capacity for pain, tolerance, and to love. Believe me, as a new widow your capacity for all will be tested over and over again. You will continually be challenged and you must remind yourself that you can - and will - be responsible for your well-being. You alone will control your destiny.

Capital gains - If for some reason you need to liquidate your portfolio to provide funds to live on, you will be required to pay capital gains taxes. No one wants to (or should) pay more taxes than are absolutely necessary. Please talk to a financial consultant or accountant about your options.

Cards - You will get many bereavement cards. A tendency is to save everything and not let go. It is your final tie to your spouse. It is important; however, to move forward...save your favorites and put those in a small memory box with other keepsakes. When you are feeling sad, it helps to re-read some of the kind words that have been written and it soothes your soul.

Cash - When a spouse passes, you may have a need for cash to pay for immediate expenses. The first order of business is to withdraw money from any joint checking account and place it in an individual account. Make sure you put enough in your account to last at least two months. Usually, by that time, insurance proceeds have been released and you will have had time to speak with an accountant or lawyer about your financial future.

Celebration - Initially, it will be difficult to think of attending a celebration when your spouse has passed on. Also, it will be a few months before you want to take part in other celebratory events. Take your time... eventually you will regain your composure and venture out. Do it in your own "comfort" time frame.

Cemetery - Choosing a cemetery will depend on your personal preference. If your spouse has expressed a wish to be cremated, then you only need a funeral home or crematorium. However, if he will be interred in a mausoleum or plot, you need to contact a cemetery. Make sure you find one closest to where you will be residing so it is easy to visit from time to time. Also, read the cemetery contract. I made the mistake of ordering a headstone that was not permitted and a compromise had to be made. In your time of grief you do not need to be distracted with little nuisances.

Change - To say that your life will change is probably the understatement of your life. Mentally, physically, financially, and spiritually your life will be ripped and torn in many directions. How you react to those changes will make the difference in how you survive. First and foremost take a deep breath and be prepared for life to get hectic. Remember ... life always changes, change is necessary to grow, and without change life stagnates. If this becomes your mantra, you will open up your mind to the transformation that follows. Some changes will be good, some not as promising. But your attitude can, and will, make the difference. There is a prayer that I say every evening since the death "God, grant me the serenity to accept the things I cannot change; the courage to change the things I can, and the wisdom to know the difference". These are powerful words and should be heeded.

Charity - There are many ways to get involved in charity. I chose to give some of the money gifts back to charities that I thought my husband would have liked to support and one that made a distinct difference in his life. Additionally, I have made it a point to get involved in charity events... it has given me a presence in the community and allowed me to meet many new people while supporting great causes. When selecting a charity, be sure to pick one that has some meaning and interest to you, as this will be an opportunity to channel your energies and take your mind off your grief.

Cherish - Cherish memories but cherish life more. Devote your time and resources to finding out what will make you a happier, more vital person. You must live your life as if this were the last day... if you take that attitude you will be reluctant to wallow in self-pity or waste time on petty problems. As a new widow, I learned a valuable lesson that is with me today. I do not keep company with people I consider have a negative aura about them and I refuse to do anything that makes me feel uncomfortable. Life is too short... live it to your fullest.

Children - If you have children it will be most important to attend to their needs. In your grief you will want to shut everyone out, but this is impossible when children are involved. Their age is not relevant; all children need a mother's gentle touch. My children were in college when their father was killed. It took my son five years to finish the healing process and my daughter still wishes for her father. Both had different reactions to the death and both grieved in their own way. What I tried to give as their mother was my love, support and wisdom. I sat up many nights with them trying to make sense of a senseless death and I continuously reminded them how much their father loved them. It is vital that children talk about their feelings. We still reminisce about the good and bad times... those memories still bring a smile to our faces. Writing a family journal can be helpful. It is an opportunity to record each other's thoughts and feelings, and help your family on their personal healing journey.

Chocolate - I have always found a good piece of chocolate, a cup of chocolate flavored coffee, or chocolate ice cream can offer some relief to a suffering soul. When you feel the blues coming on, have a cup of chocolate flavored coffee and go for a walk. You'll find your spirits lifting as you walk.

Church - A place of worship is a comfort stop for all. It does not matter what religion you are or even if you are currently practicing. Houses of worship can be powerful places to find solace and comfort. A simple phone call to your priest, minister or rabbi can ease a troubled mind. It only takes a minute to reach out to God, know that He always listens and responds. If you were used to going to services with your spouse it may be more comfortable to go with your family or friends at first.

Class - A teacher once told me "class doesn't have to advertise". People with class know that the quiet things one does in their life earn dignity and respect. In death the same principle remains. You do not need a three-page advertisement about the death. Remember that your spouse wants to be remembered for the good things he brought to your life and the lives of others. True class allows for dignity in dying and beyond. And another thing I learned along the way: you can have a first class funeral and life even if you are broke. People with class know this; people without class cannot learn.

Classes - This is the perfect way to begin getting on your feet. Take some classes. I took tennis and golf lessons and a pottery class. To this day I continue to investigate any new program or class I think I might like to try. I have learned innovative things (investing, landscaping, and decorating) as well as put my grief on hold while I took the classes. If there is anything you have ever been interested in now is the time for you to get going and enroll in a class. You will love yourself for doing it and be amazed at how much you can learn. This process also provides you with a sense of purpose, routine, skill building and takes a bit of courage venturing out alone. But it is also a wonderful way of taking you from a twosome experience to a group experience.

Cleansing - You must cleanse your soul after a death to live. Release the personal demons and despair to find happiness. This is not easy. I gathered all my husband's clothes and gave them to Goodwill (I did keep one sweater, my favorite). I called friends to come and take the tools they wanted. I donated to charities that I thought he would have wanted to support and I talked to God; He helped me see that my husband's death was not the end but a new beginning for me. Cleanse your heart and soul and learn that God will provide a way.

Clothing - The first thing I did was to gather my husband's clothing and gave them to Goodwill. I knew he would have wanted me to share with others. Do not think that keeping the clothes in a closet or a drawer will keep you closer to the departed. It stops the healing process. You need the closure and by donating to an organization that can use them, you are providing a way for your husband's legacy to live on. Since my house burned down eighteen days later, the donation proved to be timely.

Comforts - Upon death, many comforts, previously taken for granted, may come to an end. A stay-at-home mom may have to go back to work. Someone retired may have to downsize to stretch the dollars for survival. It may not be a pretty picture and you will be afraid of what's around the corner, but this time also comes with New Hope. You will learn how to do more with less. You will look to simple things to offer you solace. When my husband died, I lost a vital man who also contributed a large paycheck to our lifestyle. I thought my life was over, but after working with insurance people, stockbrokers, and assessing what I could live without; today I live a comfortable life. I did come to realize one thing: true comforts can only be found in non-tangibles; people. There is not a dollar on this earth that can provide true happiness or tranquility. That comes only from within.

Commemorate - How do you commemorate someone's life? My children and I still do it weekly with fond and silly memory sharing. After initially shunning his favorite places, we now visit them and use the time to relive some of the great times we shared as a family. And finally, a trip to the cemetery allows me to spend some time with his spirit, while planting some favorite flowers.

Compensate - How does one compensate a death? If you have insurance it will pay benefits to the spouse, but remember most people are underinsured. I learned that the hard way. My husband always thought insurance was foolish because a young widow could always marry again. Well with the cost of living the way it is there is no way that a widow could survive. What can you do? Make sure you know what liabilities you are going to have when your husband passes. Are you going to live comfortably or are you going to have to compensate by seeking employment, (or worse) additional employment, and/or raiding your savings just to get by? There is no reason that a woman's lifestyle should change because of poor planning. If you appear to be heading that way, see a financial counselor to help you set up a life plan.

Conversation - There will be times you do not want to converse with anyone and there are times when conversation will make you feel better. You be the judge of when it is most comfortable to carry on a conversation. I learned there were times I did not want to rehash the accident one more time and I seemed to put myself in a cocoon to avoid the continuous small talk. This gave me the energy to come out of my shell at other times. It helps if you carry on, through thoughts, to converse with your spouse. I still talk to my husband about the things I am feeling and how things are going in our lives. It makes me feel that he is a part of our lives, even if only through a one-sided conversation.

Counselor - A visit with a counselor can often work wonders and may be the only thing necessary to get your life back on track. Most women have a stigma about consulting a mental health therapist, thinking people will think her weak. I can only tell you of my experience and it was positive. Because of the way my husband died, and the entire trauma with both the accident and fire, I experienced Delayed Stress Syndrome. I met with a wonderful woman who put me back on the right track. She assured me that life would get better and that this short time in my life would pass. She was right.

Courage - It takes courage to be a widow. Many women are unprepared for this new status and completely at a loss as to how to deal with it. Pick up your chin, blaze a new trail, and show that you are a survivor. It takes courage to manage this new lifestyle, to make small and large sacrifices and to get back in the saddle and be a role model for your children, but you can and must show your courage. Good luck.

Credit cards - The first thing you should do is cut them all up except for the one you will use for emergencies. Now you will not be tempted to put your day-to-day living on a card that may exceed your ability to repay. If you have unusually high credit card balances, consolidate your cards to reduce your payments. Learn to live by cash only. A thing to remember: if your husband has credit cards in his name and they are part of the estate debt, you may not have to pay them back. If the estate has sufficient assets, then they will have to be repaid. Please check with your attorney.

Cremation - If your spouse wishes to be cremated a funeral home or crematorium can take care of all the details. Usually there is a showing or service and the cremation is private for the immediate family. The ashes can be buried in a plot or scattered over a favorite site. It usually is smart for the husband and wife to agree in advance on a comfortable burial method.

Cutback - No one wants to face the prospect of cutting back one's style of living. Unfortunately, most widows do face temporary to long-term cutbacks. How do you handle this? You face the task realistically and make what changes you must. I knew one widow who refused to turn in an extravagant leased car, sell her house, or go bankrupt with over $80,000 of debt, all because she did not want the neighbors to think that her husband was a bad person. This is not the time to live in a fairy tale world. Real life will dictate what must be done. You must have the determination to find new alternatives for living and existing in your changed surroundings.

Culture shock - Many new widows find themselves in a culture shock situation. Where once you had country club memberships, fancy cars and trips, the New World may not be so friendly. When the lifestyle goes, so do many friends. This is the time to start anew, purge friends and situations that will be uncomfortable for you. There are so many new and exciting friends and activities waiting right around the corner. Take advantage of this time to explore new horizons!

Pat Nowak

D

Dating - This is *always* the culture shock of the century! If you have been married for several years as I was, you are a nervous wreck. It is almost like reliving your teenage years only - the rules have changed and you missed that class! My first date was quite nice, he was a gentleman but I was still on edge. When we came home after a lovely evening, I wanted to jump out of the car before he pulled into the drive, as I did not know how to handle the exit. I really did not have to worry, as he was very polite. But there are things I have learned about dating. First: wait until you are ready. It is important that you learn to live alone before you get involved in a relationship. I waited a year and a half, but a year is a good rule of thumb. Second: do not size up every date as a potential mate. Learn that a date means a date and let things go along naturally. Have fun. Do not try to manufacture a long-term commitment. Lastly and most important, be yourself. If you are comfortable with yourself, don't allow a man to remake you into someone you do not want to be. Some ways to find men are still the library, grocery store, school, and social activities. Places to avoid are the local bar scene, the personals, and the Internet.

Daughter - A daughter is a miniature you. More than likely she was the princess in the family and the apple of her father's eye. When her father dies, so does her hero. Remember, even in your grief, you must pay attention to her needs. Depending on her age, she can be included in day-to-day decisions. You must allow bonding time each week. My daughter and I went furniture shopping, worked on refinishing one of her father's toolboxes, and went to see movies together. We also used the time to talk about her dad. We reminisced about the good and the not-so-good times. It is important that a daughter remember her father as he was, even with imperfections. We are still close today, but the foundation that was laid after the death was the cement that holds our love together.

Deadlines - After a death there are deadlines to which one must adhere. Probate, social security, taxes, and insurance claims all have deadlines. Make sure you are aware of all the deadlines and make a mental note to have what is needed at your fingertips. I suggest you get yourself a large erasable calendar that you can add or delete information, as you need it. Additionally, be sure to create an easy-access filing system. If your children are old enough, explain to them what you are doing and where to find things.

Death certificate - You will need several death certificates, as just about every agency you deal with will require an original. Make it a point to order at least twenty and there is a fee per certificate. Trust me… you will use them all.

Delight - After a spouse's death, a widow finds very little to delight in. You see despair, anger, hurt, but not delight. What does it take to push aside the despair? Every day do a small mental exercise. Imagine how empty your life would be without the beauty around you and then concentrate on how much you love it being a part of your life. It can be a walk on the beach, a sunrise, or something simple such as an ice cream sundae. It doesn't matter what. Keep adding a special moment each day and soon you will start seeing more delight in your world and less hopelessness.

Denial - Several widows I have known have lived in denial that their lives have changed. They refuse to get rid of his clothes, change his room, etc. It will <u>not</u> get any easier later. You must take stock of your situation immediately and denial is not an option… reality is the only way you are going to overcome your grief and go forward with your life.

Denigrate - It becomes very easy to wear your heart on your sleeve and make your grief public. Many widows (especially when their spouse had a few flaws) feel this is the time to denigrate him to friends and relatives. Your dirty laundry becomes public and it seems to make you happy; however, people can now use you as their cocktail conversation. Learn that your life together is sacred and left to memories, both good and bad. If you have to say anything, concentrate only on positive things.

Despair - There is great despair associated with death. If not, everyone would want to die. The reality is that to heal properly, you must cast aside the despair and slowly pick up the pieces of your life. You need to take baby steps, slowly adding new projects, people, events, and joy until one day you notice you have spent less time thinking about the death and more time on your living. You will now be able to see the light at the end of the tunnel and life will begin to turn around for the better.

Detachment - A new widow often uses detachment as a way to hide her grief. By detaching from friends and events that they shared together, she believes she will be immune to further pain. This is not the case...your inner being controls the pain and hurt; an event or a friend cannot. This is the time you should embrace your friends and concentrate on placing yourself in new situations to start on the road to healing. When you start to feel like you are detaching, call a friend, make plans with family, but do not allow yourself to shun the world and stagnate.

Difficult - There is no doubt about it: death is difficult. It thrusts even the most secure world into chaos. It forever changes lives. How do we make the difficulty less traumatic? We learn to slow down; take this time to calmly deliberate. We seek help when needed and we learn to open our hearts to people who can comfort us. There is no need to suffer alone, as there are options available. Use them to help you through the difficult stages.

Dignity - What is dignity to a widow? It is the ability to face any situation that the death has caused with quiet resolve, inner peace, and a firm commitment that you will be okay. My husband's death was played out in the newspaper and television. It became a sideshow but I was resolved not to let it interfere with the showing or funeral. When someone asked about the accident I gave what I considered a good answer and I never allowed people to manipulate me into saying more. You are responsible for you. Trust your intuition to give you clues as to what to do... and act accordingly!

Diplomacy - A new widow needs to learn diplomacy early on. Funeral arrangements will bring in-law intervention. Friends will always be offering advice. How do you handle it? You thank everyone for their kind suggestions, but insist on doing things your way. I learned by allowing my in-laws to be a part of the funeral process - even though I made the final decisions to suit my desires - I had fewer headaches and more harmony with them after the services.

Dishonest - A new widow gets a crash course in dealing with dishonesty. In your grief your will be fair game for unscrupulous insurance agents, accountants, bankers, relatives, and brokerage houses. Men (if they think you are vulnerable) will show up at your door. Do not enter into any agreements unless you seek the advice of two people. Call your Better Business Bureau to investigate all people with whom you are dealing. Be careful of men bearing gifts. This is your future on the line. Do not allow anyone to destroy it needlessly. And remember: if you need to get tough, GET TOUGH!

Disperse - There will be many financial needs to attend to after the death. Dispersal of funds for funeral expenses and an accounting for future necessities will have to be done. If you are not a financial genius consult an accountant or attorney who can help you to understand the many intricacies of probate and setting up a financial household for one.

Doctor - Do you have a doctor you can trust? Often, he is the first person you can consult when you are feeling the despondency. He can recommend a course of action and assist you in finding additional help, if needed.

Downsize - Downsizing need not be a disaster. Most women are reluctant to face the fact that they no longer need a big house, two cars, etc., but this is the time to weed out the things that you don't need and make lifestyle changes. If you have a large house, a condo may make more sense (it did for me). If you live in the country, a change to the city may be timely. Be open to change; it will help you make progress in your life.

Dreams - Pay attention to your dreams. Dreams often contain messages from our loved ones. They might also offer some solutions to the numerous decisions facing you during this time. Please remember not to use sleep as way to run away from your problems. You can make some sense of the death and learn to live a new life. It is just a dream away.

Drugs - Many widows find solace in prescription drugs and alcohol. *Do not replace one problem with another.* It will be hard to face life alone, but drugs and alcohol cannot help. If you need sleeping aids for a week or two that is fine, BUT make sure that you wean yourself as soon as you can. As for alcohol, limit yourself to no more than two drinks a day. This is a good rule at any time, but most certainly now as a new widow.

E

Eat - There is no need to tell you that when someone dies your eating habits go to hell. It must be a female thing. Either you overindulge in junk food or you starve yourself. It is important that you take notice of what food you are consuming and make sure you are getting the nourishment needed to be healthy. My habits were hardly exemplary as I ate a tin roof sundae every night for six months for dinner. But I did try to eat sensibly at other meals. Many widows will either gain or lose, after the death. While usually this is temporary and as your outlook gets better the nutrition situation will get back to normal, do not depend on it. Be aware of and control your eating habits.

Education - If you are faced with a decline in finances, it may be necessary to explore employment of some sort. If you are untrained, you may want to consider getting an education to bolster your earning power. There are many ways to finance your education with state and federal funds, special grants for older students, and opportunities to skip some classes because of life learning experience. Talk to a student advisor. These professionals can lead you on the right path for educational opportunities and remember it is never too late to begin your education!

Embarrass - There will be many embarrassing moments as a new widow. How to introduce yourself, talking about the death, simple conversations that end with tears, all play a part in your feeling self-conscious at times. Take heed, you are not the first one it has happened to and you need not apologize. Just take a slow deep breath and start over. Most people are kind and understanding. Do not worry about those that are not.

Emotions - You will go through a wide range of emotions...think of a roller coaster ride. You will be numb, shocked, angry, scared, in pain and yearn for the past. Many of your emotions will overlap so it will seem as if you are in a fog. This is a natural response. Give yourself permission to mourn; by acknowledging your emotional state you can overcome your grief and reinvest in your future without your loved one.

Employment - If employment is a necessity, make all arrangements to be ready to get the best job available. This may mean taking a few refresher courses, getting a top-notch resume together and talking to an employment assessment counselor about which jobs are most suitable. It also means competing in a younger world. This means taking a good look at your work wardrobe and updating where necessary. It means being willing to pound the pavement and not getting discouraged if a job doesn't pan out. There <u>will</u> be something for you. Trust that the job will find you, but you must help this happen!

Encourage - You are going to need lots of encouragement as a new widow. Let your friends and family pamper you a little. You must also learn that if you have a family you will have to encourage them on occasion. My son was in the middle of getting a masters degree in counseling and lost his way. I knew that if he did not pursue it, it would be lost forever. I encouraged him to finish his thesis, even though he encountered much more difficulty than expected. One of the Christmas presents I cherish the most, is the first hardbound copy of his thesis - dedicated to his mother who hounded him to get it done.

Energy - After the funeral, you will be drained. You will not want to see or talk to people. You will want to curl up in a ball and let the world pass you by. Your energy level will sink to 0%. This is the time to make sure you are eating right, taking vitamins, and keeping a regular schedule. If you find yourself sleeping too much, walking around in the same clothes 3 or 4 days, or staring at the walls... these are danger signs. To beat away the depression, give yourself a good talking to, call a friend away or consult with your doctor.

Enjoy - It will take time to enjoy life again. Tears will come easier than smiles in the first few months. You can, however, find things to make your life more lighthearted. Rent some funny movies, go out to dinner with good friends, and read some Erma Bombeck books... lighten up your heart and pretty soon you'll find more things to take pleasure in.

Enrage - The death will enrage you. How dare he die, how dare he leave you alone and stranded. How can you go on when the only things you wanted in life were to be a wife and mother? No one plans on death and no one can stop it, but you can channel your energy to other places to alleviate the rage you feel. Volunteer; spend time with your family, take long walks... let the bad feelings move through you.

Enthusiasm - Most widows, who cope with a death best, do so because they face the changes with enthusiasm. Death is not something you planned on and there will be many changes in your life, both good and bad. How you handle the changes will affect the rest of your life. If you accept change and show enthusiasm for the future, you will have a much easier time. Take my word for it... most changes in life actually turn out for the better.

Escape - How does one escape the pain? Faith, hope, and charity. *Faith* that your world will change for the better, *hope* that you will see the light at the end of the tunnel, and channeling your energy through *charity* to give back to others. This and prayer will help you escape the despair!

Esteem - Your esteem takes a beating at death. In most marriages the husband is the chief income earner. Now, all of that has changed and you are left holding the ashes. Do not under any circumstances allow your self-esteem to be damaged in this life changeover. Talk to female friends, or to a mentor who can help you see your own self-worth. This is the time to grow in original ways. Take advantage of it!

Evening Star -The Evening Star allows you to dream. I use it to meditate, commune with the wonders of nature and wish for something good. Use this time for quiet reflection.

Events - Events will go on in spite of your grief. Weddings, births, graduations, all continue to come. The world does not stop because someone dies. The quicker you can get back to celebrating the events of the living, the quicker your mental attitude will be on the road to recovery.

Exercise - The perfect way to challenge your new lifestyle is to embark on an exercise program. I did not believe in exercise but after the death I took tennis and golf lessons and started an exercise program. I found that the more time I devoted to exercise the less time I was wallowing in self-pity. Believe me, there are exercise programs for everyone ... just experiment until you find the right one for you.

Experience - Death will be an eye-opening experience. After the death, I found I had little tolerance for stupid nuances that meant nothing. I also eliminated seeing people in my life that were pessimistic and depressing. Life is too short, so live it as though every day may be your last. Look to experience life in new ways and see things, as through the eyes of a child, for the first time.

Experiment - This is the time to experiment. You are now a woman alone. If you want to add a dash of color to your life, you can. If you want to change your hairstyle or home decorating, you can. Be a bit daring and allow your own creative personality to emerge. I think, when you see some of the results, you'll be pleased. Experiment with life... good things will happen!

Ex's - Many women are faced with former wives, in-laws, or children from another marriage. Often the liaison may not be the most harmonious, but remember the showing or the services are not the time to bring up old grudges. Maintain an air of dignity, smile and be gracious. Hopefully, they are only showing their respect for the deceased. And if not, your obvious good manners will diffuse the situation. Remember nothing good ever comes from spiteful encounters...take the high road.

Extravagant - You may find, after the funeral that you want to be assured of spending money as before. Before you spend a dime, think about the expenditure wisely. Are you trying to soothe you soul with extravagant purchases? If so, the object will not make the death any easier or you any happier. Use your dollars wisely and leave the excessive purchases to a later date when you are feeling more stable.

F

Face value - You must learn to take things at face value. It is too easy to mistake what someone is saying or doing on your behalf. A new widow often perceives (quite wrongly) that people do not feel her pain and when they get on with their lives, she feels abandoned. Take what people say or do at face value, they do not mean to hurt you. But like them, you must also move on with the healing process.

Faith - You must have faith that your life will get better. Faith is not a tangible thing so you must trust that a higher power is watching out for you and will help show you the way out of your grievous state and on to a normal life. Take a moment each night to talk to God... and have faith that He will be there for you.

Falter - There will be times when you will falter; tears will come quickly. You take one step forward and three steps backward in the grief process. This is to be expected. Just when you think you have it all together, you hear your husband's favorite song on the radio and the roller coaster ride begins again. It will get better as time goes on. Time has a way of healing

Family - Your family will be your strength; and you must be theirs. Your children, parents, siblings and in-laws will all rally around you at this time. There will be little annoyances; there always are. Please remember: they will need you as much as you need them. Death will affect each in a different way. Gather around, circle the family wagons, and allow yourself time to close the book gently. Words about in-laws... keep them close. Allow them to have access to your children. They will cherish the connection and you can continue to be friends forever.

Fashion - Now is the time to change your fashion personality. Many woman dress to please their spouses; this is the perfect opportunity to create a new you. I am not talking about a bizarre, radical change, but you now have the chance to change details about yourself and clothing is one way to do this. Use your creative juices and follow your heart.

Father - Your father can be an incredible source of strength and comfort. Most women, at any age, are still their daddy's little girls. Let him console you as he did when you were a child. It makes a world of difference. I was not so fortunate because my father had several strokes and could not express what he wanted to say. I saw the look of confusion and heartbreak on his face, but we could not communicate as we should. Allow your father to be there for you.

Favorite - As a new widow, you will learn how important life is and to develop favorite little habits, which get you through the day. Mine are a flavored cup of coffee, sitting in the loft reading the paper, and being with my grandchildren. Get into the habit of spending some time, each day doing one of your much loved things. Eventually, it will become important that the thing is done and soon you replace sadness with your favorite activities.

Fear - It is right to feel fear. When you face your fears and conquer them, you are truly on the road to a better life. Financial, relationship, and lifestyle fears are all genuine and must be reckoned with, but remember there are professional people out there for advice. A wise widow understands it is imperative to seek help when needed.

Fifth Wheel - After the dust has settled you will want to venture out. There are times you will feel uncomfortable around old friends. Their married lives go on and you are left without conversation about your marital love. They may feel uneasy with a newly single woman around. Who can say what goes through the minds of people? You do not have to put yourself in a situation where you feel like a fifth wheel. Surround yourself with the friends you do feel at ease with and start to weed out the others. As you go along, you will find other people who are in the same situation and you can explore new relationships.

Financial - Most women's financial picture changes upon the death of a spouse. Some are left with insurance but no real means of supporting oneself (especially when the husband was the chief income earner). Be prepared for a change in lifestyle and do not get discouraged. Consult with a professional to discuss your financial well-being and make recommended changes. The sooner you come to grips with these changes, the easier and less cumbersome they will be to handle.

Your financial well being will be important for your future

Flirt - The first time you feel as if you might be ready to date is the first time you will have to go back into your feminine bag of tricks and learn the art of flirting. Believe me; I have flunked it many times. Being in the business world I had worked hard at earning a reputation for being straightforward, direct and honest. Making small talk and "fluttering my eyelashes" really was a new experience to me, and I am still not very comfortable doing it. There are millions of relationship articles in magazines... pick one up, when the time is appropriate, to help you along the dating way.

Flowers - Flowers die so rapidly that you may want to specify that the money spent for flowers are sent to a favorite charity or to a scholarship fund if there are young children. But later, flowers can also lift your spirits, so whenever you are feeling blue, buy yourself a bouquet or pick some flowers from your garden. My husband loved to send me flowers; the hardest moment for me was not to get flowers on Valentine's Day, which came two weeks after his death. The tears came periodically and without warning throughout the day. I learned that on each special day, to pick up a small bouquet for myself "from him"!

Focus - After the death, your focus must be on healing both spiritually and financially. Your efforts must stay focused on you and your children. By directing your concentration, your inner resolve to go forward will be paramount, and the healing process will take less time. Focus your energies... you'll be ahead if you do.

Foreclose - If you are unable to pay your mortgage, a financial institution can foreclose or take your home away from you. However, most lenders do not want to displace a family, especially one that has just had a loss. If you feel that you are unable to continue with this debt, talk to representatives from the lending organization. They will usually help you to get back on your feet; either by refinancing or temporarily lowering your payments until you get your financial plans together.

Forget - It will not be easy to forget the pain of a death. There are constant reminders daily. You do not have to forget; you must rise above the pain and go forward. To do that you do need to forget some of your past life and clear your mind to make way for a new life. Your past goes on as cherished memories and special moments that live on in your heart.

Forgive - When your spouse dies, you are angry. How could he leave you? What did you do to deserve this? The sooner you get over your anger, the sooner you can forgive what has happened to you and get on with living. To this day, I still get angry, when there is a special event and my husband is not here to share it. You will have these feelings also. The best advice is take a deep breath and think about other times when he *was* present. Also, know that he is there in spirit for every event.

Friction - A little friction may settle in when things do not go exactly as planned after a death. At this time you may get angry, blow up and say things you will regret. Take a deeeeeeep breath (and many times you may have to take several) and assess the problem. Make adjustments, if necessary, and find the solution. At the present time, the less friction in your life is better for your mental health. Some give-and-take may be necessary for this to work!

Friends - These are the special people who will give their hearts to you and are there through thick and thin. I had one couple who drove twenty-four hours from Florida to be there for me. The genuine outpouring of support, both through the funeral and after the fire, was monumental and is appreciated to this day. I keep in touch with all of my friends. They are my source of comfort and I urge you to keep in contact with your friends weekly. Give them a call, invite them for a visit or dinner, and see what true friendship can mean in the healing process.

Funeral - This is truly the last formal good-bye to your loved one. Take this time to plan a ceremony that he would have loved. Incorporate familiar touches with traditional meanings. To this day I still am fond of the little things that made this spiritual day meaningful to us personally.

Pat Nowak

G

Gamble - Life can be a gamble (so will some of your new choices), but don't gamble your life away needlessly. Do not make reckless or uninformed decisions that may jeopardize your future. The most important thing to remember is that you are now responsible for your future; no one else. Get the right information, make prudent choices, and you'll be rewarded handsomely. Document your information and date it. This can be reviewed later or compared to any new information you receive. This gives you safer odds to make good decisions.

Garden - A garden can be the most peaceful place in the world and can do much to lighten your worries. After my fire and move to a condo, I thought my gardening days were over. However, I found delight in simplifying my garden area and spending time revitalizing the condo courtyard where I live. Additionally, I found that it is fun to create personal floral space for my friends and gardening activity allows me to forget my troubles. If you don't like to garden, no problem, there are many gardens and parks you can stop by and enjoy for an hour or two...relax and smell the roses.

Goals - It helps to set goals for yourself. Start small at first, adding more as your confidence grows. If you set attainable goals, your self-esteem will soar as you reach each milestone. The sky is the limit...dare to set the bar high!

God - When your spouse dies you are angry with God, even if just for a short time. Understanding His decision is difficult for you, but you must believe that this is God's master plan for you. Do not turn your back on Him... He will always be there for you and a simple prayer will always open His door. Use this time to find peace with God.

Grandchildren - What a delight! To see life through the eyes of a child is such a gift! Grandchildren are there to make sure you do not become too somber about what has happened to you. In your grief, make sure you save time for them. Allow them to make you smile and giggle in delight. Walk with them on a beach and enjoy their awe when they find a seashell. They can make your world a more peaceful place, so enjoy them to the fullest!

41

Gratitude - Many people will extend their hand in friendship. Express your sincere gratitude often for the kindness that people will show, no matter how big or small. A simple thank you often makes another's day. Say it meaningful and often. I have been rewarded many times for the small gratitude I have expressed. Try it, it will make you smile!

Gravesite - Visiting the gravesite for some is cathartic, for others an unwelcome reminder of what has happened. Make the gravesite a personal reflection space for you to visit your loved one. I have used flowers and seasonal decorations to make the area comfortable. It does not take much to make the space come alive with a personal touch, and the time spent often allows you to discover some inner peace.

Grief - How long does grief last? For some, forever; for others enough time to get through the process and on to a new life. Only you can gauge how much time you'll need. A word of help: you can never go back to what was. Concentrate on what is and what can be and allow yourself a time to grieve and a time to heal...then get on with life!

Guardian - If you have young children, you may want to think about guardianship of your children in case something should happen to you. It is not a welcome thought and you may already have a will, but now is the time to review every decision you made as a couple to see if those decisions are still relevant for a single person.

Guilty - Whenever there is a death, the surviving person feels guilty. I know I felt awful for days, thinking I could have somehow changed the situation. I beat myself up with "what if" and "why" for weeks. This is not productive. There is nothing you can do or could have done to prevent the death... start your living process immediately and without guilt.

H

Habits - Now is the time to develop new habits. If you ate at certain restaurants, go to new ones. If you vacationed in the same place, explore someplace else. For the moment it will help you to establish new habits. Once you feel at ease with the adjustments you've made, you can slowly add the old. You will most likely find you will not need them and you are quite comfortable in your new space.

Handkerchief - Keep plenty on hand for the funeral and for every special occasion afterward. You never know when you will need them and it sure helps to have them handy. When my daughter married a year after my husband's death, I took a whole box and was ready for the inevitable. When my daughter came down the aisle on her brother's arm she was beaming. While waiting for the ceremony, they were telling magician jokes - their favorite word for their father. I never used the tissues at the wedding.

Happy - Yes... you will be happy again, but no one can tell you the exact timetable. It may take months, quite possibly years. From experience, I would say that you will start to feel more like yourself within nine months to a year. All you can do is to face each day as it comes, say a prayer, and take pleasure in the life's simple things.

Harmony - Allow harmony to enter your life. Chaos and disruptions are not good for someone undergoing trauma and grief. Eliminate people, places and things that will disrupt the inner harmony you are trying to build.

Heart - Your heart is broken. How else can you describe the situation? I like to think that it is temporarily malfunctioning and it will be fixed. Take the time to allow your heart to mend. While you are mending, allow yourself to experience the beauty and wonder around you. If you open your heart to small pleasures... the big ones are sure to follow.

Heaven - When someone dies, you will question whether there is really a heaven and, if there is, has your dearly departed indeed gone to a heavenly reward. I like to think my husband fishes in the mornings and goes to the Vegas room in the afternoons. Do I believe in heaven? I think so. But you need to make that decision for yourself.

Help - You are going to need help. DO NOT BE AFRAID TO ASK FOR IT. No matter what the problem, there is a solution and someone you can go to for help. It is not necessary to become a martyr. Help is just around the corner. It is the brave heart that knows when to ask.

Heirlooms - What does one do with heirlooms when a death occurs? If you have to downsize, you feel guilty about having to get rid of the special things from your past life. I had a different problem; my past life went up in smoke. But I learned a valuable lesson. The only heirlooms necessary are your memories and the living in your life. A chair or table will not make you feel any more or less whole, but the fond memories will. Give heirlooms to your children, grandchildren or a charity so that they can be used in their lifetime. Let them live on for others!

Hobbies - A great way to while away the hours is doing something you love. Now is the time to explore all of those things you always wanted to do but never got around to doing. I took ballet lesson, pottery classes, and developed a love-hate relationship with golf. I found that when I concentrated on these hobbies, I wasn't thinking about the grief. This process is successful... try it.

Holidays - For the first year the holidays will get you down. The traditions you shared will come back to haunt you. My children and I made new traditions. The first Christmas, we all went to Barbados and had a wonderful trip. The fresh choices made it easier to develop new traditions that fit better into our lives. Do not be afraid of change; it is often for the better!

Honesty - Recognizing that it is important to be honest with yourself is the first step to a healthy recovery. You can hide your head in the sand but it will not change the situation. The best way to recover is by being brutally honest about your situation and then looking for the right solution.

Hope - We all have hopes. When we married, it was to live happily ever after. Now at death those hopes have been dashed. We now must find New Hope that our life will be just as good as or better than before and we must trust that a higher power will help us find our New Hope. Do not get discouraged.

allow the child in you to embrace life with New Hope

Hug - You will find that a hug will always make you smile. Be the first to put out your hands and welcome a hug because giving and receiving is instrumental in the healing process. Once hugs become a habit, be sure they become part of your routine greetings.

Pat Nowak

I

Ice cream - Ice cream was my comfort food. An ice cream cone (Baskin-Robbins Butter Pecan or Chocolate Almond) could lift my spirits immediately. Use something soothing to comfort you; there is no harm in feeling good. Whether it is a great cup of coffee or enjoying the sunrise, you need not feel guilty about enjoying small pleasures.

Independent - Now is the time for all new widows to declare their independence. It is the first day of the rest of your life and it will be up to you to provide for your security. Gather the help you need and make intelligent decisions. You will feel so good the first time your choice is productive; you'll wonder what took you so long to test your wings.

Idle - Idle time makes it easy to flounder in self-pity. I am not saying you need to fill up your life 24/7, but I am saying you do need to be doing something to keep the demons at bay. Try reading, hobbies, or visiting friends; these will all make the idle time disappear and the sadness along with it.

Imagine - Imagine all the possibilities that lie ahead. Just think where you can go and what you can become. Imagination is the key to your success. Start a journal of the things you want to do and make notes on what is necessary in order to accomplish your goals. Every day or every week, as time allows, complete one task towards your goal. Soon your imagination will get the best of you and your dreams will come true.

Immediate - There are pressing needs that will require your immediate attention. The funeral arrangements, you and your family's future, must take precedence. What you need to do is to push back any petty problems that can be put on hold. Concentrate on the big issues. You'll find the little things work out for themselves.

Important - You are the most important person at this time. You must take care of yourself mentally and physically. You must face reality to make plans for your future. All other concerns should be eliminated for the moment. Be emphatic and firm that when petty concerns arise, you will not have the time to address them. It is all right to put them aside for now.

Include - You will want to include family and friends in your life. However, that does not mean they want your continued inclusion in their future. If you begin to feel uncomfortable, it is time to take your leave and find new people that allow you to grow towards your new foundation.

Inevitable - Death is inevitable; we all die someday, but how we handle others' deaths will help us recover our sanity and embrace life. Whether your spouse dies after a long illness or in a sudden accident does not make it any easier. What is inevitable is that you must continue your life. What will make it easier for you is to recognize that it is important to start the healing process at the funeral. Only then can you bravely face what comes next.

Inflict - Many widows inflict needless pain on themselves. They feel that acting like a martyr will allow people to feel sorry for them. This gets old real quick. You need to learn there are two kinds of widows... the "self assured" and the "victim". While self assurance can only be attained through a trial and error period, you will still be much happier than assuming the role of a victim. Victims never really learn to stand on their own two feet and continually fall prey to unscrupulous actions that continue to allow them to remain victims. Allow nothing to stand in your way of gaining the self-confidence you need to grow and move forward.

Information - Information allows you to make careful, prudent decisions that will affect you and your family. Do not go unarmed into any situation without the necessary information needed to make the proper decision. There are experts, the Internet and the library, all at your fingertips, to help you find the information you need. Make sure you use the tools at hand; you'll be glad you did.

In-laws - Most marriages come with in-laws and in death that relationship technically ends. If you have had a rocky relationship, don't think the death will erase that. However, my advice is to be as cordial as possible both during and after the funeral proceedings. If there are children involved, keep the in-laws in the picture and if there are post-probate proceedings make it a point to inform them. I am still in contact with my in-laws and it has allowed my children to enjoy their paternal heritage.

Insurance - Make sure that you are aware of what insurance is available after the death. Don't be surprised and wake up to find yourself destitute because your husband had inadequate coverage or let the policy lapse. The number one reason for insurance is to provide the living with a comfortable lifestyle, but the reality is that few people actually have enough insurance. As a person who was left in that situation, I am here to tell you, that if your husband refuses to address those needs in advance, you must!

Integrity - An individual goes through life with two key elements that set him or her apart from others: class and integrity. I have found that people do not need money to have class and a person's integrity can be detected immediately. Handle any proceedings with as much class as you can. If there are difficult periods, make sure you hold your tongue, do not rise to bickering or engage in silly arguments. Allow your integrity to set the stage for how your life will proceed.

Interview - If it is necessary to seek employment, an interview may be needed. If you have been out of the work place or in need of seeking a better job, it is important in the first meeting to set yourself apart from the competition. Use friends as a networking base to begin the search. Brush up on interview techniques; practice in front of a mirror. Take the time to learn about the company you are considering. These are things that will help you land the job. Additionally, be sure to invest in a professional resume.

In testate - If your husband dies without a will, he has died in testate. This means you will be sharing his assets with your children and any others who want to come forward with a claim. I urge all women to investigate what provisions have been made for their future and insist a proper will be executed. Remember, upon his death, your will must be changed immediately to make sure your wishes are met.

Intuition - I always found, as a new widow, to trust my intuition; and I was right 85% of the time. I trusted it most when dealing with people. If I did not feel a bond immediately, I sought another opinion. If I felt uncomfortable about the situation, I went with my gut feeling. You must also. Do not underestimate your natural instincts to determine a dangerous liaison. Trust your intuition!

Irresponsible - This is not the time to act irresponsibly. You need to seek professional opinions for major things that need to be done. You and your family's future depend on responsible actions. Do not act in haste and consider all ramifications before making a final decision.

Irrevocable - If you and your spouse had done previous estate planning, you may be faced with irrevocable trusts that will need to be discussed with an attorney. Make sure you are comfortable with the person you choose. Seek advice from a family member and/or a trusted friend when choosing this professional.

IRS - As you are well aware, the IRS does get its due. You are still responsible for getting any tax forms together and making sure the estate pays its taxes, if necessary. A note of advice: you may file taxes as being married during the year your husband passed. After that you are placed in a higher single tax bracket. Consider making immediate tax saving plans with your accountant. The best time to do that is before you become a widow!

Irritations - There will be many irritations and they will magnify under the circumstances. Every small incident will make you react like an erupting volcano. You may be short with family or friends and you may act surly. This is part of the grief process. When you think you may overreact, take a deep breath, or excuse yourself for a moment to get your head together. People will understand. Minor irritations need not make a beast out of you!

J

Jealousy - Jealousy will rear its ugly head, at times. You may feel it when you see married friends and long for that special time again. You may experience it if your lifestyle changes and you no longer can afford the luxuries your friends have. For a while, do not place yourself in a compromising position to be jealous, and if you are unfortunate enough to find yourself in that position, get away as soon as possible. One note of caution: when your children meet a new beau for the first time, they will experience that same feeling (comparing him to their father). Encourage them to express their opinions, so that you can discuss things openly. Jealousy is an ugly word and you must be strong to rise above it.

There will always be awkward moments............put on a smile and make the best of it.

Jewelry - When is the moment you take off your wedding ring? You will know and it will differ from woman to woman. Your time of realization will come with no fanfare; no advance warning. If you were given several pieces of jewelry, I encourage you to continue wearing them, as a symbol of his love. What I did was to keep my favorite pieces and on every special occasion (the birth of my grandchildren) I redesigned some of the other pieces to give to my daughter. This way each piece can live on through her.

Job - If you are employed when your husband passes, you will find your job offers you an escape, for a time, each day. When you are a busy worker, your mind does not have the time to wander to your problems. Most places of employment are very sympathetic about allowing an associate time (if needed) after the death for critical meetings. However if you are faced with the need to seek employment, make sure it is where you are going to be happy. There is no point to finding a job that makes you miserable. This compounds your problems, adding more stress to an already precarious mental balance and is not good for the curative process.

Jog - This is a great way to get rid of stress. Take a jog around the park, through your neighborhood, or down a jogging path. If you haven't jogged before, start slowly. Remember to warm up and take off on a path that can lead you to new adventures just ahead.

Joke - You may think you will never smile again. You will, even if it takes a while. Laughter makes you feel better and jokes can go a long way toward getting that smile going. Go see a funny movie, rent a great video or get a book that makes light of life. All will help jumpstart the humor. Humor is a great resource for helping the body heal.

Journal - Many new widows start a journal. It helps them express private feelings that they do not want to make public. I started one, but I soon found myself not devoting the time to write and eventually I put it aside. However I learned that journalizing may take shape in many ways. This book is my journal; a way to help others through their passage to a new life.

Journey - Life is a series of journeys; the paths have many peaks and valleys. You will find in life that the most important thing is the journey, not the destination. Here is where you make your life choices and have the opportunity to explore different paths. Once you reach the destination, remember to begin another journey or you will stagnate. Cherish the small pleasures that come along your way as they will be great memories. Also consider putting together a picture collage, which can be a way of documenting the importance of milestones along the journey.

Joy - Joy for the immediate period of time will be suspended, but will return. It is necessary to find the joy that exists in small moments, as these small moments become the better part of your day. Take a walk in the park, marvel at the sun, moon and stars; spend time with your children and grandchildren. Allow yourself to find the joy in life; it will not find you.

Junk Food - Many new widows exist on junk food. They are no longer cooking for two so it just seems easier to pick up a bag of potato chips to eat. Immediately get into the habit of making yourself a meal, even if it is a microwave dinner. Now is not the time to abandon healthy eating habits; you will need them more than ever.

Justice - There is no justice in death. Obviously no one wins and it seems everyone loses. However, justice can be served if you immediately set a course for your self-preservation. It will be imperative that you face the future with continued optimism and a will to survive. With this attitude, you will be on your way to a successful new beginning.

Pat Nowak

K

Kaleidoscope - Your New World will be like a kaleidoscope. One day you will turn the scope and find calmness and serenity, and the next day, fire and brimstone. The roller coaster ride will continue for some time so get used to the ups and downs that will rule your world. If you remember to take the stages with baby steps, the jolts may not be as earth shattering.

Keepsake - Many new widows want to save every keepsake. Every letter, gift and piece of clothing is ferreted away as a "remembrance". Objects cannot make your life less miserable; they may only clutter it and weigh it down. Your memories will allow your loved one to live on. Pick a few pieces that are your favorites and make them your keepsake. The rest can be given to your children or to a charity in his name.

Karma - Your karma is destiny. Do not think that you could have changed the death in any way. You are not responsible for it; a Higher Power predestined it. If you understand that from the beginning, you will heal more quickly.

Kids - My kids were my saving grace. They kept me on my toes and watched over me. We planned activities and events that kept us busy and we shared in our grief. If you have a family, make them your priority at this time. It will be good for all of you!

Kind - I was amazed at how kind people were to me. My friends and workmates were always popping in to talk, planning activities, and making sure that my needs were met. When my house burned down, my employer planned a house shower to furnish my new condo. I was in shock but I still remember and cherish all the kindness shown to me. If you are so fortunate, remember to thank your helpmates. Simple thanks do go a long way to help friends know you appreciate their support.

Kiss - After you have that first date... at some point there will be the first kiss. No doubt about it - butterflies will be flitting in your stomach. Don't feel you have to rush the dating and relationship process. Take time to first know who you are and what you want in life before pursuing the first kiss.

Knowledge - They say a little knowledge can be dangerous, but in your situation you are going to need a lot of knowledge to help you make intelligent decisions for your future. Make sure you get the help you need to proceed and to process the knowledge necessary for a secure future. Do not be afraid to ask if you are unsure; this is your future that you are now taking responsibility for.

L

Laughter - They say that "laughter is the best medicine" and it certainly is. I can remember laughing with my children over some of the funny things that transpired when their father was alive. It sure helped the healing process. Just because a person died does not mean he never lived. If you remember the humorous, as well as the serious, you will find yourself moving forward faster.

Library - I spent so much time in the library. I used it to take out books to occupy my time and as a learning source for the many things I questioned. These days, you can rent videos and DVDs, get tax information and join reading clubs. There is a great New World waiting for you at your local library.

Life - Life is for living. When someone dies your life gets suspended in space. You do not know how you will survive and, therefore, perhaps it would be better if you died too. Remove that thought immediately from your head. There is life after death and it is for you, the living. You have another destiny to fulfill. The quicker you learn this, the easier the transition will be. A word of advice: the funeral is the end of one chapter and the beginning of another for you.

Light - There are days when you will think there is no light at the end of the tunnel. You see so much darkness and despair. Say a prayer, chart your course, and find your own light. It is out there; all you need is a little courage to begin the journey.

Limbo - Limbo will seem to be your fate several times after the death. Dealing with insurance, social security, pensions, human resources departments, etc., will always be a source of agony. How do you get out of limbo? Have all your facts and necessary paperwork available and in order for these agencies to do their work properly. Make sure you meet deadlines for responses and call first thing in the morning since most agencies get busier as the day goes on. Put together a calendar of important dates, meeting times, and names. These will all make the adjustments easier.

Livelihood - The money left to you either through insurance, stocks, or savings will be what you use to fund your livelihood. Now the trick is to have enough money to continue on with your lifestyle, uninterrupted. If this is not going to be the case, you will be faced with decisions for your future welfare. Is employment or house downsizing eminent? These are questions you need to answer. The sooner you explore your options, the sooner you'll be able to plan for your future. Start now!

Lonely - It is hard to imagine life without your spouse and you will be lonely. How do you face each day when there seems to be no reason to go on? It is very easy to fall into the trap of allowing your loneliness to get the best of you, but if you allow that to happen eventually it will be difficult for you to see any hope. Plan your life so you have very little time to be forlorn. There are plenty of opportunities waiting for you. Volunteer, take a class, visit hospice patients or just go for a walk...once you see how good you feel, the loneliness will fade away.

Love - Certainly you loved your spouse; will that love ever come again? Who can say? Many women go on to remarry and find themselves just as happy. Some will never marry again. Your future is uncertain, but be open to the changes around you. I found that I needed time to adjust to being alone and I waited to date. You will know in your heart when it is time to go on that first date and on to a new loving partner. A word of caution: never compare your new love to your past spouse. Both relationships can be wonderful, but they will be different. No two people are alike, nor should they be. You certainly are not the same person you were prior to the death...recognize those differences.

Luck - You will need a little bit of luck to see you through. Although, at death, you will think your luck has run out, you will find times that, just when you need it, something will happen to ease the pain. I was amazed at how many times a thoughtful word, an unannounced check, or a much-needed gift would arrive to make my day. Cherish the small-unexpected treasures that luck brings.

M

Magic - I maintain that when someone dies there are instances when unexplained happenings occur. I have marveled at how many strange things took place after my husband's death which, to this day, remains a mystery. At first I tried all kinds of rationalization to decipher the meaning, but I came to realize, rather than try to explain it, I like to think that angels are working their magic to make the transition as easy as possible. You might want to consider that same thought. There is nothing wrong with having a little magic in your life.

Maintain - How do you maintain your sanity when your world is crumbling before your eyes? You say a prayer, you talk to a mental health professional or you visit a friend. Make a pact with yourself immediately that you will do whatever it takes to help you get on with your life. Do not veer from your course. If something has to change to maintain normalcy, prepare yourself for that alternative!

Makeover - After my husband died, I spent time on me. I opted for a shorter haircut, changed my hair color, strolled up to a counter at one of the department stores and got a makeover. The changes were not earth shattering, but I remembered how good I felt after the experience. Make a moment for you. Most makeovers in department stores are free and you are not obligated to buy anything. Changing your hair color, beginning an exercise program, or revamping your wardrobe are all little ways to begin again. Spend some time on you!

Marriage license - Just as with death certificates, make several copies of your marriage license. Everyone will want proof that you are indeed who you say you are. Have several copies ready to mail, as necessary.

Medicine - Chicken soup is good soul strengthening medicine and so are many over-the-counter products you may need for a short time. Stay away from prescription painkillers, anti-depressants, and sleeping pills. It leaves you in a drugged state all day. This part of your life must be faced with a brave heart and a clear head. If you need some medicine for the moment, choose something over-the-counter or ask the pharmacist for advice.

Meditate - There are a great many meditation exercises that cleanse your soul and allow your spirit to be set free. I know yoga and Ti Chi are two that are meant to reach in and reduce stress. Go to a bookstore, get a feel for what's available and ask a learned salesclerk for advice. Then go to the library and check them out. Once you've read the book, you will know if this is something you want to pursue and you can go back to purchase the book for your personal growth library.

Meet - As a new widow your life will transform. Some friends will fade away and you will meet new people to take their place. Concentrate on church activities, local social and school events, and casual get-togethers with work associates or friends. Stay away from the bar scene. There are plenty of places to meet people who share something in common with you. Investigate and you will find new friends just around the corner.

Melancholy - You may feel melancholy for several months. You will not be able to put your finger on the feeling because it may come and go. The worst times are usually early in the morning and late in the evening. Your mind has time to stray and it tends to pick up on all the inequities of life. If the entire day has been so-so, it becomes worse because while misery loves company, you have none. What you need to do in the morning is to plan your day so you do not give yourself a chance to bring up useless feelings. In the evening, make sure your hours are packed with enjoyable activities so that you literally fall into bed, ready to sleep. Do this for a few months and the pattern will be set. There will always be a bit of sadness, though, at special events... and this is to be expected.

Memories - Oh, what memories you have! Regardless if you have been married a short or extended period of time there is a myriad of memories about your loved one to save. Many women wonder if they will forget in time. No, and there will always be something that will trigger a memory, either happy or sad. Memories are there for life. Remember your loved one fondly. Never be ashamed or embarrassed about your memories.

He is there at your side in spirit...............cherish the memories

**Mom - **If you have a family, you are a MOM. Do not push your children aside during your grief. This is the time to embrace them and continue as a family. It doesn't matter what their ages; they will need you in different ways. Young children will not understand death; teenagers will have lost their parent and young adults will no longer have a friend and mentor. They will all face the death in a different manner and each *needs* a MOM to help them through.

Money - Money will be an important factor in your life after the death. Lack of money will change your future dramatically. You may be faced with having to downsize, or seek employment. This will add more stress to your already beleaguered life. If you have an opportunity before the death, investigate your options. Make plans to obtain more insurance or talk to a financial planner. They can provide you several ways to plan for the unexpected. If your husband has already passed, get all your documents together and forge a plan of action you can stick to. Decrease expenses, consolidate bills, and seek help from agencies that offer assistance and do not get discouraged. There will be light at the end of the tunnel (and it is not a train); it just takes awhile to see it.

**Morning - **Each morning will be the start of another day without your spouse. There is no doubt that it will be difficult to face the morning. Upon opening your eyes, say hello to God and start to plan your day. This will help prevent your mind from wandering into self-pity. Get going immediately and make exercise a morning ritual. In time, you will learn to love the mornings.

Mortgage - Your mortgage is what is owed on your place of residence. Some people carry mortgage insurance, which will assure that the house will be paid for if your spouse dies. This, of course, will offer you peace of mind in one area. However, if the house is going to be burdensome with taxes and home expenses, this is the perfect opportunity to sell and look for something more affordable, thus giving you savings to invest. If you do not have mortgage insurance, then you will be responsible to pay the monthly bill. If there are going to be payment problems, it is wise to discuss this with your mortgage holder, as early as possible so they can advise you as to what can be done to help you. If you are up-front with them, they will be helpful to you.

Mortuary - If your loved one is ill prior to death, and you have some notice that the end is imminent, you may want to investigate the mortuary where funeral proceedings will be held. Just as with any service you are considering, ask specific questions about service and rates. Make sure you are clear about what you want and need. If you are uncomfortable, try another place. If your husband passes suddenly (as mine did), you may wish to choose someplace close to home as I did. It proved to be just the right place for me. They offered kind, considerate staff and, even after the funeral, called to see if I needed anything further. This time is hard on you. Try to find a mortuary that will make it as easy as possible.

Mother - Just as you are a Mom to your children, your mother is there for you. She can be a quiet source of sympathy while offering an ear to listen. Just like when you were five, most mothers can help the hurt, just a little. Talk to her today!

Music - In death as in life, music can soothe your soul. As music fills in the quiet, it allows you to think. Put on a great CD and allow music to transport you to another place.

Mystery - You will discover that death is a mystery. You find yourself with questions such as why him and not me or what could I have done to see this coming. This is the true mystery of life. There is no rhyme or reason as to who is taken and when. You have to believe that this is all part of a Master Plan that remains a mystery to us while we are alive, but will someday be clear.

N

New - Everything about life is going to take on new proportions. It will all be frightful and scary. Change is always difficult, but the way you handle it will cause you to either grow or stagnate. Make a vow to yourself that the new changes will not daunt you and you will be a survivor!

Neighbor - If you have neighbors, they can be a source of comfort. "Make new friends, keep the old"; is a little nursery rhyme that continues to be important. Keep in touch with your neighbors.

Nest Egg - It would be wonderful if we were all left with a nest egg that would allow us to live comfortably for the rest of our life. If this is the case, wonderful, use it prudently. If this is not the case, make a promise that once you are on your feet some money will be saved to provide you with a retirement nest egg.

Night - Just as in the morning, the night often finds you facing those ghost monsters under the bed. Plan activities until you are so tired you literally fall into bed. If you still find yourself unable to sleep, keep one or two compelling books on hand to pick up and read. Usually, this is all you need to doze off and keep the negative thoughts away.

No One - It is important to learn that no one else is responsible for your life. It will be up to you to make choices, chart a path, and continue on living. No one can look inside your soul or heart and interpret your feelings. I made a pact to take one day at a time and face every obstacle with quiet determination. It worked and allowed me to grow and change. Now I owe no one...and it certainly gives me inner pride in my accomplishments...every woman needs that feeling.

Nourish - There will be people and things that nourish your soul. Surround yourself with these exclusively. By eliminating people and places that breed negativity, you allow yourself to grow and flourish. Take a hint and choke the weeds, but nourish the flowers!

Pat Nowak

O

Oasis - There will be an oasis or a place of relief. It may be your church, a favorite coffee house, or a nearby park. It can simply be sitting in the sun in your backyard. Go to that place when you are feeling blue. Usually, a visit to your oasis is the only thing you will need to make your heart feel a bit lighter.

Obituary - An obituary notifies people of your husband's death. If your husband was prominent, it certainly may be news. Accept the fact graciously that in that case, the obituary is for the public, not the survivors. Such is the cost of prominence. I have found that for most people a simple obituary is best. A litany of prose will not bring him back; let the memories be personal for all.

Obligatory - In death, there will be many obligatory proceedings that will need attending. This may take its toll on your spirit and you may find yourself tired and depressed. Get plenty of rest and face each meeting with a resolve to learn something from the moment. By eliminating the negative thoughts early on, you may find yourself not dreading as much as you thought you would.

Oblivion - Many new widows are afraid that their spouse will fade into oblivion. Out of site, out of mind is usually the way life is. I have found that everyone has their own special memories of your spouse and those memories will allow him to live on to all, in different ways. He will not fade away into oblivion.

Obsess - Women are obsessive by nature. Trust me; it gets worse when your spouse dies! You beat yourself up trying to think of ways you could have saved him. You obsess that you did not do enough while he was alive, and on and on. Take a deep breath and ask yourself, in the great scheme of things is this going to matter? If not, throw the thought out. You need not worry or feel guilty; death is part of living for us all.

Occasion - The funeral is certainly not a happy occasion, but you can fill it with wonderful aspects that will make it meaningful and allow people to remember his life, rather than his passing. Find the perfect balance; I am sure his spirit will be watching!

Offend - With your fragile disposition, someone may say, or imply, something that may offend you. Do not rise to the transgression. Take a deep breath or walk away. You are very sensitive and vulnerable right now. It is so easy to speak regrettable words that will come back to haunt you. Listen, learn and speak softly.

One - This is who you are now... one unique person responsible for you. Until you marry again your new designation in life is one. What you make of that oneness is up to you. I chose to make my single state a time for me to discover who I was and what I wanted to accomplish. This new exploration can be a mind opening revelation... so please make the most of it!

Opportunity - There will be many new opportunities at your disposal. Why not explore an opportunity for a new career, mind expanding activities, or go back to school. What you do not want to do is squander the time on self-pity. Seize the moment and every new opportunity with the wide-eyed amazement of a child. Your new life can be fruitful, if you let it.

Organize - Organize and prioritize your life after the funeral by making yourself a daily list and using it as your bible. This will allow you to keep the needed balance. With so many things going on you cannot afford to have things falling through the cracks. Even if you are not considered organized, this is the time to develop fresh habits that will serve you long after death matters are cleared up.

P

Pace - It is difficult to know how to pace yourself when someone dies. You race around thinking you must be an accountant, lawyer, counselor, and super mom to your children, when it is best to just slow down and pace yourself for the long haul ahead of you. There will be mounds of paperwork, phone calls, meetings, questions and lots of tedious chores. If you take things as they come, you will be better off. Don't get overwhelmed. Everything will get done in time. And most important... do not forget to put aside some time for yourself.

Pamper - Women, by nature, do not like to pamper themselves. Always doing for others, most women are running on near empty. This is now the time to pamper yourself. You will now have that moment to get a manicure, read a book or explore a new hobby. I had a great time learning new things and exploring my inner self. I actually found I enjoyed some activities I never thought I would. Go on an adventure; you will be surprised at what you will find right around the corner.

Panic Attack - Do not be surprised if at times you feel like you are spinning out of control. This is a panic attack and it will happen occasionally as the process becomes overwhelming. My first panic attack came the morning after the death when I realized I was totally alone. It was so frightening. I learned that panic attacks are a myriad of thoughts that all come together at once to overload your brain, which then causes the panic. You must take a deep breath, bring your heart rate down, and then break up the panic process into manageable areas. If you concentrate on only one thing that needs to be done and push the other thoughts to one side for a moment, you become more focused and less apt to lose control. Panic attacks will last for a period of time so the earlier you learn to manage this, the better for your mental well-being.

Paper - You will never see so much paper in your life. Paperwork for everything: death, social security, insurance claims, etc. You will have nightmares about all the things you need to fill out. A word to the wise: make sure you are aware of what all the paperwork is about, and how it will affect your future, before signing. If you are unsure: ask, ask, and ASK!

Parents - If your parents are alive they can be a source of support. You can, for a moment, be a child again and allow them to console and guide you. If your husband's parents are alive, this will be a difficult time for them. A parent never wants to see their child die before they do and many never get over the shock. I was very sensitive to my father-in-law's grief and eased his pain as much as I could; but my future - and that of my children - had to be more important to me than his...be responsible for your needs first.

Park - A place filled with serenity. I made it a point to spend as much time in a park or park-like settings as I could the first year. The change of seasons, the quiet solitude, all energized me and allowed me to go on. Pack a picnic lunch and stroll down to a neighborhood park and let nature introduce the wonders around you.

Partner - Your spouse was your partner in life. Your marriage was easy because you knew each other so well. You could anticipate needs and moods... and this was a good thing. Will you ever find a partner like this again? Some will; some may not. All you can do now is to learn how to take care of yourself. Once you're on your feet again, love may or may not come, but now you will be able to handle what comes your way with confidence.

Party - The first party you are invited to will be difficult...even before you get there! You will procrastinate and make a multitude of excuses for not going. For a while, you are going to have to force yourself to have fun. That will be hard. The first party I was invited to was the night that my house burned to the ground. Had I been home I probably would have tried in vain to save what we had. As it turned out, I was not there and was spared that part of the agony and frustration. If you have a chance to have fun, seize it!

Patience - This virtue will be practiced until perfect during the months after the death. Waiting for people to answer your requests and filling and re-filling out forms will all take its toll on you. You will find yourself wanting to be rude... and biting your tongue to keep from saying what is really on your mind. Practice patience. When you find yourself ready to say something unthinkable, concentrate on something that makes you happy and the ill feeling will pass. This will be a good lesson for life.

Pets - Pets are an enormous sense of comfort. They seem to know what is going on even though they are not human. Our dog was inconsolable. He and my husband were best friends. After the death, he would not eat or sleep in the bed. I was so eager for him to be okay. Unfortunately, he perished in the house fire just eighteen days later. Though I was distraught, I knew he went to a better place. In an eerie twist of luck, one year later to the day of the death, we found a dog of the same breed, abandoned at the church where my husband's funeral had been held. The dog would likely have perished that night as the temperature dipped to -15 degrees. Today that dog is alive and happily living in a warm and loving home with me. God does work miracles.

Pension - If your husband has retired, you are entitled to the pension he earned while employed. The thing to remember is that some pension rights may be discontinued after remarriage, so check with your husband's employer to learn about everything you are entitled to and what options you have. A corporate Human Resources department is usually very obliging and will try to ease your concerns with helpful answers for your future.

Perseverance - Another virtue that will be needed is perseverance. There will be many times you will think you are beaten down and cast aside by the system, but you can persevere. I did. My problems seemed insurmountable at times. Insurance claims, homelessness, and a lawsuit to file... but I found that as I completed each task, I became stronger and more resolved not to be a victim. What I learned is that just like the little engine who could, you can and will persevere!

Pictures - I was lucky; my pictures were saved from the devastation. While they smelled of smoke (and still do) from the fire, I cherish them more than ever. Where else can you find the legacy of your life and a chronicle of your existence? Pick out your favorites and display them; or put together a family album that you can look at from time to time. It does help the healing.

Poetry - I saved a few poems that I received after the funeral and put them with my family albums. Many of the poems in the cards still sustain me today. Put one or two in your bedside drawer and when you need a lift, read them. If you are so inclined, write some yourself.

Positive - It will be difficult at this time for you to look at life positively. Whenever we are dealt a traumatic blow, we tend to become cynical and focus on the negative. This is the time to cast away those negative thoughts and concentrate on the positive things that were and will be. You must immerse yourself in actions that focus on positive energy and help you to readjust to your new role. Do not think for a moment that it will be easy, but it is something you can accomplish. You will be amazed at what positive energy can do when you believe in happy thoughts!

Pragmatic - At this time it is essential to be pragmatic about your future. Now is not the time to alter your thought process. It is important that you do nothing foolhardy. Make sure all decisions are rationally thought out and discussed with professionals. A simple lapse of memory can often spell disaster and this is not the time to add to your problems. Consider all options before making any decision.

Prayers - What an opportunity this is to talk to God and let Him know your feelings! Ask for His help and blessings and let Him show you the way. It need not be in a formal church setting, any place will do. He will help and guide you. Your prayers are powerful communication tools.

Presence of mind - When your children were young and had some minor crisis, like most mothers you had the presence of mind to know what to do to make things better. You will need that same quality... only magnified several times. This is the time you must think and act as clearly as ever, because this is your crisis and how you manage the situation will be crucial. Analyze the situation, talk to a trusted friend, and initiate a solution. It will put your mind at ease and allow your future to be secure.

Probate - Every state has different probate laws. Check with your attorney to find out what is needed to probate your spouse's will. If he died without a will, this may present some problems for you, because you will have no clear-cut ownership of his assets. A good attorney can help you through the process and ease the burden. Better yet, this discussion should take place with your attorney while you are both alive.

Psychologist - At times the grief can be overwhelming. Rather than suffer in silence, as many women tend to do, call and make an appointment with a specialist who can help. Two or three sessions with a professional often are all you need to get back on your feet. Most visits are covered by health insurance, so please do not be a martyr. No one likes to listen to a complainer who does nothing to help alleviate her own problems.

Purpose - Death often finds a new widow questioning the purpose of life and, more specifically, her life. At this time, she sees that she has nothing, is nothing, and can see no rainbow. This is the time for your own personal pep talk. Stand in front on the mirror and tell yourself that you will be responsible to find your purpose in life. It is no longer a case of relying on someone else to qualify your life. There are two options: you can make it your purpose to be all you can be in life, or just continually be a casualty.

Pat Nowak

Q

Qualify - Upon death, you may have to investigate to see if you qualify for benefits and options. At times you will think you are a scavenger. But trust me; no one just comes forward to throw money or assets your way. You need to explore every option and find out how you qualify to receive this-or-that benefit. You may find some nice things under all the rocks you turn over.

Quality-time - It is so easy to squander time. We always assume we have all the time in the world. But that's not so. You have a certain amount of time on earth. Make sure all your time is quality-time. I made a promise when my husband passed that I would not waste time on negative people or issues. I have kept my promise, which meant removing me physically from some comfort zones. I found, in the long run, that I enjoy my life so much more living it to the fullest. Make your choice quality time, every time, and all the time!

Questions - You will have a myriad of questions. My advice: either ASK for what you need or visit a library and LEARN what you need to know. All your questions do have an answer, just look in the right place, your answer awaits you!

Quote - Many women have an "I want it now" attitude. I was used to calling and getting done what I needed immediately. One of the hardest lessons I learned was to get several quotes when I needed a service performed. On one specific occasion I found I could have wasted several thousand dollars if I had not bothered to call and get several quotes. After this incident, I became a believer. Do not accept a single bid without checking the competition. It is now your money; don't squander it.

Pat Nowak

R

Rage - Your rage will be uncontrollable at times. You will want to yell, scream, and throw a tantrum. Life is not fair and you are the victim. Every widow feels that way; this is normal. It is what you do with your rage that will allow you to go on. Do not turn it inward. Do not become a bitter victim spewing venom about the unfair situation. Turn your rage into a positive outpouring of energy focused on helping others. If your husband died from cancer or a heart attack, volunteer with those organizations to reach out to other potential victims and survivors. Make his passing a private crusade to better your life and possibly others. It will be a tribute to his memory.

Rainy Days - Rainy and gloomy days have a way of depressing you especially in light of the situation. At these times put a little sunshine in your life. If the weather is calling for rain or snow for an extended period, organize an indoor picnic for your grandchildren or friends. Make plans to attend your local museum or volunteer at school. You need to keep yourself occupied, so the trick is to make your own sunshine.

Reaction - How you react to any situation is tantamount to your well-being. Death is a sobering reality check, reminding us that we are not immortal. Many women become a hysterical mess, unable to manage the simplest of tasks, while other women calmly get through this period and save the trauma for their private time. Our personality make-up is what determines how we react to personal situations. If our reactions are hysterical by nature, death will magnify this severely. Remember hysterics do not help the situation. You need to stay calm to respond in a purposeful manner. Just keep telling yourself to take one hour at a time. When my husband died, I shrieked like a mad woman upon hearing the news, but then talked to myself to get under control. I found that I thought and acted more responsibly when I was thinking clearly. It also helped my children with their reactions.

Read - I found that I became a voracious reader trying to find as much information as I could about the problems facing a new widow. Magazine articles, law books, etc. all filled my time. Reading helped me find solutions for many problems that were lurking around the corner. Make it a practice to read what you need, but also read to take your mind off the situation. Reading can take you away from reality for while. Often, that is just what you need; a respite from the reality of death so that you can recharge yourself for what is ahead.

Rebound - How long does it take to rebound after a death? It all depends on your state of mind. I found that within a year I pretty much was into a new routine and had made peace with the situation. I also made a pact to start immediately after the funeral to get my life together. Many women never completely get their lives together and that is sad. Your life does not end when death takes your spouse. Remember that you need to pull yourself together and get a survival plan ready for action.

Record - It is essential to have a record of every part of your life. Birth, marriage, and death certificates are needed and, if you are like me, I had records scattered helter-skelter. I was always searching for a needed paper for this-or-that. This is the perfect time to start impeccable record keeping and organizing your files. As you need it, create a file and put it away. Then when tax time comes or an insurance question looms, you are prepared and it is easily accessible.

Refuge - Where does someone find refuge? There will be much advice from family and friends but the real question is: where can you go to get instant shelter? For some women it will be a place of worship, for others a quiet evening spent with friends. For me it was a walk in the park or at the beach. There I could clear my mind and find instant peace. It allowed me to marvel at God's creation and know that there was a plan somewhere for me. Find your place of refuge and allow a bigger force to help you heal.

Embrace family and friends..........you will need them for future healing

Relationships - You will find your relationships will alter as your life changes. Friends for years may fall by the wayside, as you explore new friendships. Your late husband's family may fade from the picture. As you begin to date again, a whole new existence will open up for you. Be open to the changes in your life. Only then can you grow as a person. Make it a habit to live each day as if it is your last, with no regrets about past associations.

Religion - Often religion has been an integral part of our daily lives and now, with death, it can play an even more important part. We must have faith and allow our belief in the religion of choice to see us through this troubling time. No, it will not save us from our sorrow, but it can open the door and allow us to use its spiritual healing for a time. God is there; just place the call.

Relocate - You may find it more prudent to relocate after the death. I know I contemplated the thought immediately. We lived on two acres with hours of yard work, and I was a novice when it came to using the lawn tractor. The maintenance on the house was overwhelming and I was all alone. On the other hand, this house was the only home my children had known for nineteen years and I could not, in good conscience, pull the rug out from under them. The house fire actually helped me make the decision; with no home left, the choice to move seemed the perfect solution. My move to a condo was an ideal choice for my children and we all love the change! Do I think you should relocate? Not immediately. Often a change of location is a great way to make a new start in life. Sometimes you may be forced to because of financial concerns. The thing to remember is that it is the people who inhabit the house that makes it a home, not the structure. Do not be afraid. Things always work out for the best!

Remarriage - In time, you may find someone who makes you feel special again. Tender feelings have aroused your heart and you are ready to make a commitment to remarriage. Remember the following: make sure there is magic. I have often said to marry again I want the magic... that breathtaking feeling that I cannot possibly live without this person. If that feeling is not there, perhaps it is better to wait a while to commit. However if the feelings are there, run to the altar and live happily ever after.

Remember - "Remember when..." it will always be a silent refrain. You can be driving down the street, listening to a melody and a thought will pop into your head. At Christmas or on birthdays, your mind will wander off to days past and your heart will ache. Other times, it will be as if your former life never existed. It is acceptable to remember, be sad, shed a tear, and laugh to yourself at something funny that happened years ago. Never forget the beauty that was your former life; remember it fondly.

Reminisce - At first it will be difficult to reminisce. You need time to get through the adjustments in your life. As you come to grips with the changes it will become easier to talk about the past and your spouse. As the year moves forward you may actually bring up some of the things he said or did without actually bursting into tears. You will know you are healing when the reminiscing becomes a part of his legacy and your future.

Repay - What do you do when you are filled to the brim with financial obligations and you have no idea where to start? You pull together all of your financial information and take it to an accountant. He will, for a small fee, make some sense of your financial future. If you need help with loan repayments, contact the lenders and alert them to the situation. No one wants to throw you out of your home or take away your car. The bank is willing to work with people who are honest about their problems. Trust that things will get better and you will find the courage necessary to formulate any financial changes in your life.

Resilience - A woman is resilient. Who else could have been wife, mother, chauffeur, cook, nurse, teacher, disciplinarian, cheerleader and always with a smile (sometimes not a big smile). Draw on that inner resilience to get you through the trauma. You, through your multiple roles, are accustomed to the changes necessary to run a household. Apply that knowledge and mental toughness to the tasks that will be facing you...once you analyze, you will find that the changes need not be as daunting as you imagined. You will be quite proud of your talents, once they are uncovered.

Resources - Where do you find the resources, after a death, to help alter your life? Why all around you! I used the library for information, the park and beach for serenity, friends for honest opinions, my family for strength, and the local ice cream store for tin roof sundaes to make me smile. Look around with awe at a perfect sunrise; take your grandchild for the day and marvel at how he sees life. Pick up a good book and read it until you can read no more. Resources exist for those willing to use them!

Respect - Respect the dignity of your spouse. When my husband died, he had several friends, many from his boyhood days, and I had several hundred because of the business I was in. I was amazed how many of these people stopped by to pay a visit. This reminded me of a dear teacher who once cautioned us in class to show respect for every human being because in God's eyes, all are created equal. Your reward will be the same respect coming back to you a hundredfold. I witnessed that firsthand and now I make it a habit to respect every person for who they are, not for what I would like them to be.

Responsibility - Your first responsibility after your husband passes is to get back on your feet. You need to use all of your resources to assess the situation, put together your life plan, and find the determination to succeed. You will need to push aside the whining, the feeling sorry for yourself, and wallowing in self-pity. This is now where you bear the responsibility and your life depends on the choices you make. The sooner you realize this, the easier the alterations will be.

Résumé - It may be necessary, for your financial well being, to seek employment. Whether you are currently working, or now need to seek work, it is most important that you have at your disposal a professional résumé. There are plenty of books to help you put together the résumé that shines. It is helpful to ask your friends to circulate it. Often it is not what you know, but who you know, that gets your foot in the door. Do not overlook your volunteer duties as part of your background. Many corporations are community minded and seek associates who are committed to community causes. Most importantly, however, look for a job that makes you feel comfortable. Money and titles do not mean a thing if you are not happy. Your happiness is what your life should be about!

Revenue - You need revenue in your life to exist and your revenues must exceed your expenses to get ahead. Believe me; unless your husband left you a fortune, budgeting will be a lifelong commitment. If your husband was the financial wizard of the family, you are now left to put together the jigsaw puzzle for your future. It is important to consult with an accountant to put your puzzle pieces into perspective. Once you have a clear monetary picture, you can make the needed adjustments in your life for smooth sailing.

Ring - You were given a ring at marriage. How long you continue to wear the ring after the death is up to you and your personal healing process. Some women wear it for six months to a year and then feel comfortable taking it off. Others wear it longer. You will know in you heart when it is time to take your wedding ring off. I allowed my daughter to design a pendant with the stone from my ring. I still get to keep the piece closest to my heart.

S

Sad - There is no doubt that happiness will evade you for a while. No matter how hard you try the sad days at first will outnumber the happy. After the death and fire I found myself drained. It is not an easy thing to get past the misery. There is one thing you must remember: it will get better, but it does take time. You will soon be aware of a few smiles coming to your face. Be proactive in seeking things to do and places to go. When you force yourself to be a part of life, the sad days will begin to ebb and disappear.

Saint - The one mistake women make is to elevate their husband to sainthood, upon his death, "he did everything right, no one could compare to his feats (real or imagined)". You are doing yourself a grave injustice by not realistically remembering the total man and reminiscing about the good and bad. This allows your children to remember the father they knew. All people make mistakes - which is what makes us who we are - so remember the whole man. We still laugh at some of the crazy things my husband did and it makes us miss the fun we had as a family. My husband also had an alcohol problem, which was not part of our happiest times. By remembering both the happy and sad we are reminded how fragile life is and how important it is to make our lives the best possible while here on earth.

Sale - Your financial situation is liable to vary and you may find yourself forced to sell your home or some belongings. This, coupled with the death, may send you into a hopeless tailspin. The sooner you realize the necessities of downsizing or "right sizing", the quicker you will be ready to face your financial situation with eyes wide open. Obtain financial assistance from an accountant and quickly make plans to get your monetary house in order. This is not the time to be despondent about the issue. The longer you procrastinate, the more in debt you become. Make haste now.

Sanctuary - After the death I was immediately hit with a devastating fire. I longed for my old house because that had always been my sanctuary from the hustle and bustle of the world. The house, in the country, had an air of serenity. Imagine being faced with eviction by an evil fire. I did not handle this well since all women do need a safe haven after a death. I ended up making do, and with patience, found the perfect new house. It was not only a sanctuary situated on a small lake, but also a place my children love even more than our original house. This taught me that home is where the heart is, and an address cannot give you a safe place; only your family can do that.

Satisfaction - There will be satisfaction when you discover you have the strength you need to get beyond the death and ahead to your new life. I look back, eight years later, with a satisfaction that I have made a full life for myself. I enjoy my children and grandchildren and have eliminated people and places of negativity. Satisfaction *can* be guaranteed; you are the one to do just that!

Savings - Hopefully your savings will sustain you until your financial picture is more certain. Upon death, remove enough money to see you through for two to three months. This will give you the monetary relief you need to pay your current debts. Within two months you will have a better financial blueprint for your future. You will also begin to receive insurance and other benefits. With 20-20 hindsight you may wish you had been included in financial discussions, but many men do not feel women should bother their pretty heads with number details. A word of caution: now that the financial decisions are up to you, learn everything you possibly can about basic household and personal finance accounting and how it will affect your future. If your children are old enough to understand, teach them too!

Schedule - Your life is now in limbo; your usual routine no longer exists. Eating, sleeping, and entertainment as two become a schedule for one. And quite frankly, you need to shake up the schedule. Instead of coming home to a lonely meal, schedule dinner with family and friends or take a class right after work. The sooner you forge a new identity for yourself, the quicker your schedule will change to accommodate your new life.

Self - Most women do not think about self. As a wife you worried about your husband, and as a mother your children's concerns were paramount. Now you are alone and self must be a priority. To heal and be a viable woman, you must discover whom you are and what you need in order to maintain and go forward. This will take honesty and inner serenity. Ask yourself what is necessary to make the rest of your life controllable and comfortable. Then set about doing it for and by yourself.

Self-confidence - Many women who are widowed actually find a fresh level of self-confidence. Once part of a duo where the man was revered, a widow may actually find her niche in life's new conquest. As a woman grows and discovers her new identity, old habits die off leaving room for a shining star to emerge. Embrace the changes and move forward with a new zest for life! Let your self-confidence take over!

Self-conscious - Just as you need to get some confidence, you also need to put away the self-conscious attitudes that may haunt you. If you were indeed the other half of a man revered, you now may think of yourself as unimportant. Your identity was completely tied to your husband and now that he is gone so is your identity. That is a cop-out. Go forward and develop a distinctiveness that is relevant to your assets and personality. What a great time to discover your talents... Happy hunting!

Self-sufficient - Probably one of the most gratifying things that happened to me was the realization that I could be self-sufficient. It did not happen overnight and I still have times when I am overcome with alarm that something can shake up my comfortable world. The inner strength you need to discover will allow you to see that you are capable of handling anything that comes your way. This is the destination where every widow needs to reach...fearless of her future.

Sentimental - Women are such sentimentalists; every love letter, card, and picture is lovingly saved. Death is hard on sentimentality. Every time you read or look at a picture, you have tears in your eyes. This is not a bad thing. We need to be sentimental to be in touch with our human side. I still get teary eyed over a wonderful card or a special song on the radio. As long as, the sentimentality does not border on depression, you'll be fine.

Sex - If your sex life as a married couple was vibrant, being alone will be a problem. You will long for the intimacy you shared in your former life. Do not look for a one-night stand or a pick-up in a bar. You will feel awful afterward. I planned activities until I actually fell into bed each night, making sex a fond memory for a while. When the time is right and you find the perfect new man, you will be ready to explore increased levels of intimacy. Please remember one thing:

the sexual habits of your former life should not be brought up. They are history and this is a new life with fresh adventures. Enjoy!

Shake-up - To say your life will be shaken up at death is really an understatement. The world you once knew no longer exists and that is devastating. Now you need to remind yourself that you have a different life waiting for you right around the corner. Where there is revelation, there is also New Hope for you.

Sleep - Your sleep patterns will profoundly change. To this day, I get up every morning since the death without an alarm clock. There are nights I still toss and turn, unable to get to sleep. Some advice: don't become dependent on sleep aids. If you need help for a short period of time, they are okay to use, but use them carefully. I found Tylenol PM® worked just as well.

Socialize - It is hard to socialize after the funeral proceedings. You find your one wish is to curl up in a ball and not be heard from again. What you must do however is to take baby steps back into socialization. Attend small social get-togethers at first followed by larger events, as you feel more comfortable. This gives you an opportunity to get your sea legs. It will take awhile; don't rush.

Social security - You may be eligible for social security benefits if your husband reached age 65. If not, then you may then be entitled if your children are under a certain age. Take note: social security benefits today are not comparable to years ago and you may find yourself with a financial shortfall if you are depending upon these benefits to live on. Check with your accountant for more clarification.

Solution - You will be left to find the solutions after death. You find your resolution once you are confronted with the problems. There will be many, some as trivial as funeral protocol, and some serious, such as your financial well-being. I found my solutions from being knowledgeable about the problem at hand, seeking out every possible source of information, and trusting my gut instinct when it came to the final decision. It worked; it can for you too.

Son - A son is the rock. He sees himself as your savior, protector, and all around hero. What you don't suspect, is that inside he is probably a small child needing to be reassured that everything will be all right. It won't matter how old he is; the same applies if he is six or sixty. You may need to allow him to vent his anger at the death, reassure him of unconditional love, and permit him to be your protector for a while. My son was always at odds with his father, nothing serious, just different philosophies that never came together before the death. It took my son several years before he realized his father truly loved him; being a man of few words, my husband let the opportunity for meaningful conversation slip through his hands. You as the survivor will have to clarify the message. This teaches us a valuable lesson: we should always let the ones nearest and dearest to us know how much they mean to us each and every day.

Spend - It will be an essential and ongoing financial task to learn what you will be able to spend in the coming years. Hopefully your husband left you comfortable, but most often that is not the case. No one ever thinks death can be right around the corner. If you are left less than rich, a good course on money management is imperative for your future. Get registered today, so you have money to spend tomorrow.

Spiritual - After death, you need to revisit your spiritual commitment. You may find it hard to believe that God is just and loving - especially under the circumstances. Nevertheless, the reality is, now more than ever, you need a strong and spiritual force to help see you through the difficult time. Do not turn your back on Him; instead embrace your spiritual beliefs.

Splurge - You may feel the need to shop-'til-you-drop as therapy. Think again, as you may need the money for everyday expenses. Before you overindulge on unnecessary purchases, make sure they will not leave you cash-poor down the road.

Star - I have my own theory on stars. I believe everyone who passes on becomes a star. I can gaze at them and make a wish. A beautiful night can often trigger those unhappy moments so transfer them into fond memories and wish on the star.

Starve - Many new widows are often unable to eat. The physical sight of food makes them ill. This is a natural reaction, as your mind and body are in shock. For your health, you must eat something. Concentrate on smaller, less filling meals and avoid fried, fatty foods that may cause some stomach distress. Fruits, crackers, lean meats, etc., are easy on your digestive system.   Besides, it is a healthier diet. Do not starve yourself; you do no one any good if you are ill.

Stocks - You have all heard of the stock market, but how much you really know may be the mystery.   I was left very little money and needed to provide for my future retirement so I took my savings and invested in stocks. While they can be volatile, they also provide more growth than other savings plans.   I talked to several people, chose a trusted broker and spent some time with him exploring the stock plan for my needs.   I also read everything I can about investing.   I have found that I actually know a little bit about what I need to do and my 401K reflects that knowledge.   Take the time to invest in your future.

Stress - You will feel the stress.   You will be stressed out. There will be days when you want to scream because everything is traumatic. You will magnify every problem until it becomes a disaster. This is not the time to go into a melt down.   Take a deep breath, go for a walk, and put away the problem for another day.   If your stress-o-meter is on high, it is best to take a break.   Just a little bit of time and space often pushes the nerve-racking situation to the background and allows you to handle it better at a different time. Do not be afraid to say, "This is too much to handle today, I will consider it tomorrow."

Support Groups - There are support groups for widows in the community.   Often a mental health group or a church will hold meetings for those who are dealing with grief. The occasion to speak with other women who have gone through the grief process is just the critical element a widow needs and the therapeutic benefit of shared experiences can help a widow with the adjustment to the death.

Surprise - It is so nice to see pleasant things transpire after someone passes.   You just have to notice the pleasant happenings. In your grief, you often overlook the niceties that happen, the little surprises.   Look around you; people are trying to make you smile. One of the nicest surprises I had after the death and fire was that the associates at my office held a new-home shower for me.   I was speechless for weeks and so touched. There will be many times you will be equally encouraged by a small surprise; acknowledge it graciously.

Survivor - After the death of a spouse, you have two choices: become a victim or a survivor. I chose survivor. Making this choice did not mean I instantly became a superhero. It meant I was willing to take what life handed me and deal with it. It means you go forward with determination and grit to make a place for yourself. It means you grow from this experience, become stronger and make your life mean something, no matter how small. Your option is to be the perennial victim, always on the receiving end of pain and suffering. You lament how life is so unfair, but do nothing to change it. The death only gives you more ammunition to continue on as a victim. The choice is yours; chose wisely.

Sympathy - It will be hard when acquaintances show expressions of sympathy. What do you do with all the cards, flowers, memorials, etc.? How do you react? Graciously. I did not have enough time to let people know where I would like donations sent so my husband received almost 250 floral arrangements. I was in shock. However, I realized that I could also make others happy. After the funeral, I dispatched almost 100 floral pieces to local nursing homes for residents to enjoy. I gave others to relatives so they would have a remembrance. I took my sympathy and turned it into expressions of love from him.

Pat Nowak

T

Take a stand - A new widow is often worked over by the system. You will be talked down to and be considered a light weight; someone not to take seriously. This is when you need to plant your feet on the ground and take a stand for what you need in order to make your life better. This is an opportunity for you to grow as a woman in charge of your life. You may not have had the chance before, but now is the time to discover what it is you need and want in your life. Make a list and do not be deterred by nay Sayers. This time it is about you. Stand up and be heard.

Talk - It is healing to talk about your spouse. Additionally, it is comforting to visit with family and friends and talk about your fears for the future. Talk allows you to express your inner torments - and there will be many. But there comes a time where we must put away the painful memories and begin talking about our new hopes and dreams. Use conversation as a good form of therapy. If communication is difficult, remember to write in a journal. Expressing your feelings is of importance for moving through the trauma in your life.

Taxes - Taxes do not stop just because you are a widow. I found another surprise when I discovered that after the death year I was taxed in a higher bracket, as a single person. Take the time to investigate the tax liabilities you will be facing. While you are not taxed on insurance settlements, you will be responsible for federal, state, and probate taxes. This is mind-boggling to the uninformed and requires the help of an accountant and attorney. Be sure to hire professionals who are skilled in estate planning programs.

Tears - How many tears do you shed? Possibly a billion. Most of them are shed the first year. But there will never be a day that you are tear resistant. I still tear up at an unexpected moment or when a cherished song or event happens. It is natural. The first few months it is advisable to have tissues handy at all times. Do not apologize when the tears come; it is a natural part of healing.

Telephone - The telephone was my mainstay after the funeral. I used it to keep in touch with family and friends. I spent countless hours ferreting out information on death benefits, insurance, etc. After the house fire, my cell phone nearly melted down with thousands of questions to the insurance companies. Use this handy tool as a means to get any and all information you need for survival.

Tense - The first six months can have you walking a tightrope, which seems ready to snap at any minute. Your body will hurt from being tense 99% of the time. This feeling comes from fear of the unknown. The death leaves you uncertain about life and your future. How to dissolve the tenseness? Investigate, formulate, and dissipate; three words to help erase "tense" from your vocabulary. Investigate your options, be thorough, and formulate your plan of action. The tense feeling will evaporate once you become more settled.

Terrify - There is no doubt you will be terrified. You have no clue as to where to start and what to do next. This thought scares the hell out of you and you will wake up nights simply petrified. This is when knowledge is power - at least over terrifying situations. Get your life back on track, investigate your future options, and make concrete decisions. You will then begin to feel in control. This coupled with constant activity and calming exercises, such as yoga, will relieve you of those frightening feelings.

Thanks - Remember to give thanks. Death may not be the time you think of giving thanks, but every day it is important to thank the people who have helped you to get through the day, in some way. Most importantly, thank and ask help from a Higher Power. You will need it and He does hear and help.

Therapy - There is a place for therapy after death. If you find yourself unable to function, living day to day in a fog, and not seeing any light at the end of the tunnel, then it is time to go to therapy. A few sessions with a professional psychologist may be just the thing you need to get your life on track. Usually insurance benefits cover this service. So, assure yourself that you are not crazy, but willing to explore any means to get back to a normal life. You will see results.

Thrifty - Since your paycheck often gets cut immediately, "thrifty" is a good word to get to know. Until you know your financial outlook, do not recklessly spend dollars you may not have. I went from a comfortable income down to a moderate income. The shock was immediate and swift. Even with insurance proceeds I knew my former life was gone. I learned some economical ways and found that I can live pretty much as I used to if I was willing to make some little sacrifices. It may be a necessity, but you will be glad you found the fountain of frugality.

Time - Time does not heal all, especially when it comes to a death. But time has a way of nullifying some of the hurt you feel. It slowly allows you to explore your future, begin a new adventure into life, and make sense from the hurt you feel. Give yourself the right amount of time to heal. It will be different for everyone.

Timeless - Your former life is timeless. Every memory, picture, and event will be forever etched in your mind and in your heart. Trust that you will never forget what was and that will help you to find what is, and can be. Take your past along to your future.

Today - Immediately after a death it is important to take one day at a time. You will need to investigate your future plans, but it helps to control your immediate panic if you do not bite off more than you can chew. Use a plan of action for each day, stick to your schedule, and you will find that as today turns into tomorrow you will be able to take on more responsibility. You will be surprised at how far you will come in a few short months by taking smaller steps.

Tragedy - Death is a tragedy for everyone. It does not matter if it was expected or accidental, it still destroys a family. What is necessary is to get beyond the tragedy? Remember what has happened cannot be changed so it is your duty to get beyond the moment and into your future life. It will not be easy, and no one will say it will be. Do not turn a death tragedy into your life's misfortune. Take control of your life and turn your tragedy into your success.

Trust - Whom do you trust? Your soul mate, who was the person you depended on and trusted implicitly, has left. If there is a trusted friend or family member, ask for his or her advice. If you need business advice, call the Legal Aid Society. They can make recommendations. It will be up to you to make the overtures, and it will be up to you what advice you chose to follow. I used a trusted friend I had known for years. He guided me and gave me some options. I did make sure the final decisions were mine; so should you. If you are uncomfortable with a suggestion, seek another opinion. This is *your* future you are dealing with so you owe it to yourself to take your time and think it through.

Trust fund - If you are left with a sizeable estate, you may want to explore giving some to your children or grandchildren. A trust fund can often be set up to help you bypass taxes and give a future to family members. Make sure you consult with an attorney or accountant skilled in setting up trusts. While I did not receive a windfall, I did give both of my children a portion of the insurance settlement to start their financial future...it made me feel good. You may want to investigate this option.

U

Unbearable - 'Unbearable' will be the word you use to describe the aftermath. You will be overwhelmed and numb with grief. You will not know where to turn. It is essential that you think positively and immediately push the unbearable thoughts or words out of your mind. It is crucial to get a grip on what needs to be done... and you cannot do this if you have negative thoughts clouding your mind. Push ahead with a determination to make your life go on in a positive manner.

Understanding - After a spouse's death, your mind does not work properly. It plays tricks on you. At this time make sure you have a clear understanding of any contracts you sign, analyze any verbal messages for clarity, and ask to have everything made crystal clear in writing. In your grief, you may do things that will create potential land mines down the road. Clear understanding avoids those pitfalls.

Upheaval - You will likely not have any bigger upheaval in your life. Nothing you will ever go through will be more traumatic than the death of a spouse. Your world will be turned upside down for some time. Getting it turned right side up will take patience, determination, fortitude, and prayer. It will be worth the effort. The more optimistic you are in facing the upheaval, the fewer problems you will have in the end. Make a "positive outlook" your mantra.

Upset - A new widow often gets upset over little things. And the more frustration you show, the more the problem magnifies. Sometimes writing a list and prioritizing the bigger issues from the smaller ones helps you to see more clearly the path you have to take. As you solve a problem, physically scratch it from your list. This feels good and you see some resolution. But a good rule of thumb is to ask yourself "in the great scheme of things is this going to make a difference in my life?" If the answer is no, chuck the problem. Save your energy for the big problems you will face.

Pat Nowak

V

Vacation - One of the best things I did for myself was to take a vacation with my children. It gave us time to be a family and heal as a family. Today, my children still refer to that vacation as one of the best they had. It helps to have time to get in touch with your inner grief. Our vacation was to Barbados; but a long weekend trip to a city nearby will do. When you are on vacation, it is necessary to plan activities and keep busy. You will be surprised at how much fun you will have. At this critical time vacations require a giant step, so be ready to take it…and take it!

Value - You may be required to estimate the value of assets that become part of the estate. I learned the hard way not to trust only one estimate. Be sure to get two, and sometimes three, estimates. This gives you leverage if the value is contested. It also helps to put perspective on your financial future. Be penny wise to avoid being dollar foolish.

Vices - A new widow often turns to some crutches to get through the day. A few drinks to numb the pain, or the prescription from the doctor pushes grief away. Pretty soon you have acquired bad habits that will do more harm than good. Believe in yourself…you can face whatever life gives you. You don't need drugs or alcohol to be a partner in misery. Instead, concentrate on activities that take your mind off the situation and keep you busy. They will be just as effective as drowning yourself in a bottle and have no negative or lasting effects.

Vitamins - Eating and sleeping habits change after a spouse dies. You may find yourself without an appetite causing your eating habits to become lax. Sleeping is non-existent and your health suffers. Be sure to take vitamins through this period. They will help to supplement your somewhat dysfunctional diet for a while. You don't need to add health problems at this time.

Volunteer - I found volunteering is a good way to get through this difficult time. By spending a few hours at local organizations that needed help I felt good about myself. It also made many of my days more bearable. How to choose that special organization? Personal choice. If your husband died of cancer or heart disease you may want to lend a helping hand to one of those organizations. Or you may have another favorite organization...any one will work. All you need to do is pick up the phone and make that first call to commit yourself. Start small (1-2 hours a week) and add more as it feels right for you.

Vulnerable - One of the hardest lessons I learned is that a widow is vulnerable to con-artists and seeming do-gooders, who really are not who they say they are. Make sure you deal with professionals, and if someone offers you goods or services that are too good to be true, most likely they are! It is up to you to take care of yourself...so arm yourself with valuable knowledge and be wary of strangers bearing gifts.

W

Wake - The wake is a time to honor the memory of your late husband. Whether or not to have a wake is entirely up to you. Some prefer the services only. Others want family and friends to gather for one last time. It also helps to add special touches that chronicle his life to the services and the gathering. Explore using meaningful pictures and heartfelt verbal tributes to make the gathering memorable.

Walk - I took many walks after the death. Something as simple as walking provides a much-needed outlet to channel grief. It is great exercise and helps you to think more clearly. It seems I could always find a solution to my problems by taking a walk. Make it a point to add walking to your list of daily activities; you may want to take a friend or family member along. Make this a priority and a gift to yourself.

Wallow - Many women wallow in self-pity after a death. Some would rather become a victim. Do not be one of them. Use this time to grow and become stronger. Use this strength as a means to find your future destiny.

Water - Water has healing powers. I sat at my pond, moved to a condo on a lake, and our vacations are often centered on water destinations. When you are lonely, seek out a quiet place around a lake and find how easily your heart grows lighter.

Welfare - Your welfare is paramount to your survival. It is up to you to seek out all the answers to insure your future will be a bright one. Many women lack the knowledge needed and throw up their hands in despair, rather than look for a solution. Don't leave any part of your life to chance... take positive action now!

Well-meaning - There will be so many well-meaning people full of advice. Everyone will have thoughts about what you need. I found it easier to smile, listen to the advice and then go about my business. I think every person means well, but certainly, many will not understand your personal situation. Consider their advice, but make your own decisions.

Whine - It becomes easy to whine about the unfairness of death. One often gets caught up in the despair of the moment and we bore our friends and family endlessly. We need to get past the anguish and channel our energies optimistically. One such way is to focus on the plans for your future. Leave the past as a pleasant memory and leave the whining out of your conversations.

Whisper - If you are very still, you might hear a rustling of the wind, feel the breeze across your cheek or think you have heard a soft voice in the house. A whisper perhaps, but I really think our loved ones have a unique way of letting us know they are around. I have learned that life will bring you many unexplained surprises...let the love surround you.

Will - If your husband dies without a will, state laws dictate how the estate is to be divided and you may not always come out in a good position. If there is a will, all of your husband's wishes for the future will come to pass. Remember to change your will, immediately, so that your desires will also be followed should something happen to you. Be sure to include a power of attorney and a living will.

Wise - You gain wisdom by gathering knowledge and using it prudently. As a widow, it becomes imperative that you make the right decisions. Consult with professionals, discover the truths you need and make your wisest choices based on this knowledge.

Wishes - As a child, we often had secret wishes. Sometimes they came true. As an adult we become more pragmatic and push childish notions of wishes from our mind. We often forget the child-like simplicity to wish. As you are embark on this new journey you need to become a child again and make wishes for your future. They don't have to be grandiose, but it does help give you hope so make a wish today!

Withdraw - Do not withdraw from living. It is easy to be so caught up in the grief process that you turn your back on family and friends. This is the time to embrace life and make a strategy for your survival. If you feel you are withdrawing, make an immediate plan of action to get in touch with your inner grief and seek family and friends for living activities.

Wonder - You will always wonder why you. Why did this happen to you? Could you have prevented it? These thoughts will tear your heart out. You need to transfer your wonder into action, much like a child discovering new adventures. This will help you adjust your mental attitude towards a favorable outcome.

Worry - Will you worry? Yes, continuously! Your whole life is now in disarray and around every corner there is another problem certain to give you more agony. What I discovered was that the more I worried, the worse I got! If I worked harder at the solution rather than worrying about the problem, I usually not only found an answer, but it was also the right course to take. I am not suggesting that you close your eyes to your problems; I am asking you to assess the situation and look for the resolution. Give most of the effort to gaining the knowledge for the end result, rather than expending it on worrying.

Write - Do you like to write? I really did not. However, I found that by putting my thoughts on paper I could see some progress in the healing process. As I grew, so did my thoughts. Pretty soon my thoughts became more positive about what I could do to change my situation, rather than a tirade on the injustices of death. Writing is cathartic. Use it to help you grow.

Pat Nowak

X

Xerox - A word to the wise. Make copies of *everything*. In fact, make three copies because you may lose one. I can't stress enough how important it is to be organized and prepared. Avoid the hassles: invest in a small desktop copier and photocopy everything.

Pat Nowak

Y

Year - I found, personally, that it took one year to feel like I was back in control. It was a year of change, growth, and enlightenment. I was amazed at how strong I had become. I learned how important it is to take care of oneself. One year is only a general rule of thumb. Don't panic for some, it will take longer than others. Do not try to rush your healing process; allow it to happen naturally. Help it along by looking for the positive energy in life. You will heal in time!

Yearn - You will yearn for days past. Your former life will be what you use to gauge your measure of happiness. It is important to let go of the past and concentrate on your future. It will not be easy to do this but some simple exercises work. Concentrate on adding a new activity to your life once a week; add another one the following week. Eventually, your past will become a pleasant memory and you will look forward to your future with anticipation!

Yes - In the beginning it will be difficult to say "yes". Friends will ask you out, events will come up and you will find yourself declining the invitations. Learn to say "yes". There is no fun in staying at home with the ghosts of your past. Look ahead and allow living to begin. And it does so by saying, "Yes, I can do that."

Yesterday - Yesterday is yesterday. Your former life is a former life. Remember that old Beatles' song? It was a pretty song... but a formula for disaster: "Yesterday/All my troubles seemed so far away/Now it looks as if they're here to stay/Oh, I believe in yesterday." There is nothing wrong with enjoying yesterday, but it is essential that you pack up your yesterdays in a memory box. They are not "here to stay." Go forward with determination for today and hope for tomorrow.

Yield - An old proverb states that if you are kind and give of yourself you will be blessed with a higher yield. This old proverb is worth remembering. If you concentrate on surrendering your grief for the betterment of others, you will be richly rewarded. It does not have to be huge; a small kindness shown means more than an ostentatious gift given with no thought. It is good to give, especially if it is of yourself.

You - The most important word to remember when you become a widow is YOU. It is *your* life that will change and it is up to *you* to make sure your emotional and financial future is secure. Take time for YOU! George Elliott once said, "It is never too late to be what you might have been". Find out who *you* are and where *you* want to go. Most importantly, learn about what it will take to make YOU happy... and then start doing those things.

Do something.............just because it makes you feel good.

Z

Zeal - You must embrace life with renewed zeal. I learned a valuable lesson after the death. Anything worth doing is worth doing for my happiness and with all the enthusiasm I have. *To merely exist is not an option.* Thoreau once said, "Most men live lives of quiet desperation." Don't let that person be you!

Zero - This is what you start with at birth and it is up to you to multiply your assets. After a spouse's death, it is a little bit like starting at zero, as you are reborn. What you make of your challenge is going to be the sum total of your determination and fortitude. The first day of your new life begins now!

Zest - What do you like to do? Now that you are reborn make sure to renew your zest for activities and friends that you never had time for when you were a couple. The world is now open to discover; take advantage of all life has to offer.

Zoo - I love going to the zoo. The animals make me laugh and the beautiful surroundings allow me to forget my troubles. Use a day at the zoo the same way. If you are too embarrassed to be a kid alone, take your grandchildren or your neighbors' children. Smile and have fun, for that's what life is all about!

FINANCES
IN A
FLASH

These pages are designed to give you a quick way to cut through the financial redtape with easy to read information that every new widow needs to know but usually travels through a maze to get to:

INSURANCE

Life insurance is necessary to:
- Allow for sufficient assets for the widow and her family to live comfortably after a death. It provides instant cash (within two months) and is tax-free.
- Provide your estate with liquidity. If you do not have enough insurance it may be necessary to sell your other assets to pay estate costs.
- Allow for continuation of household maintenance when a working spouse passes.

Types of life insurance:
- Whole life policies provide a small return on cash value and are usually more costly. However, the policy maintains a cash value and therefore can be "cashed in" at any point before it is redeemed.
- Term Insurance is taken out for a term, has no cash value, is less costly than whole life, and is needed only while you are busy building up other assets. Once you stop making premium payments, the policy stops. The only benefit it provides is payment if death occurs within the term of the policy.

Things to be aware of:

- Instead of buying several insurance policies, it may wiser to increase your existing policy amounts.
- Check if your policy is double indemnity (pays double) for an accidental death. If not, it is a small charge to upgrade for that service and well worth the money This is from personal experience as one who did not have that clause.
- Make sure your insurance policy is owned by both of you individually so the proceeds after death pass automatically to you without going through the estate.
- It is imperative after the death to deal with your own insurance review, making sure your dependents will be cared for and have the necessary money for your funeral expenses and probate needs.
- If you have credit cards or bank accounts, check their insurance guidelines. Often they carry an insurance provision on the cardholder for accidental death.

Now if you have already amassed enough assets through a 401K, stock portfolios, and real estate, it is not as important to have as much insurance. Review your insurance needs with a qualified agent or attorney.

Death Claims:

After the death, it will be necessary to contact the company either directly or through your agent. The company will be quite helpful and will walk you through the procedures. You will need to send them:

- A copy of the death certificate (and some may require a marriage certificate).
- The original policy.
- Within sixty to ninety days the company will, issue you a check, transfer funds to an account, or allow you to invest in several of their money funds.

Homeowners Insurance:

Whether you own or rent you need to have insurance. When you choose insurance, look for the following:

- If an accident should happen on your property you want to be prepared. Carry at least the minimum but more if you can afford it.
- Replacement value - it is imperative that your policy is for replacement value. If your policy does not reflect replacement value, you will lose valuable dollars through depreciation and it may not be enough to replace the property or contents. This policy acts as an inflation rider.
- If you have jewelry, art, antiques, furs or other valuables, separate coverage may be needed and is available for an additional charge. In any case, it is extremely important to have an itemized list and photos of these items. Store these somewhere safe and fireproof.
- Deductible amounts are what you need to pay before the insurance company funds will commence. If you want to keep your premiums lower, have a higher (up front) deductible.

Health Insurance:

- When your spouse dies, if you were included on his employers insurance, you may lose this benefit and will need to find health insurance for yourself. You will be covered for a short period of time under a COBRA plan (Continuation of Benefits Rights Act - a federal law that requires the benefit plan continuing to be available to you for eighteen months) but you must pay the premium. However, this is generally less expensive than any self-paid plan you will find.
- If you are employed, you can opt to enter your employer's health plan if you are not already covered by it. If that is not a possibility, it will be necessary to investigate an individual health coverage policy (often costs range from $250 to $800 per month) depending on coverage. If you are over 65 you become eligible for Medicare's Part A at no charge and Part B at a monthly premium.

Casualty Insurance:

- This insurance is used to cover your property as a liability umbrella (liabilities from claims and judgements) and health. This may not be needed if you have an automobile, health, or homeowner's insurance policy, which would cover the same requirements.

Automobile Insurance:

- This insurance protects the owner of an automobile from claims for damage to property and injury or death to persons that may happen as a result of an automobile accident. When your spouse dies, make sure your automobile insurance is changed to reflect your new status. Also, spend some time with the agent reviewing any questions you may have about the policy. Be absolutely sure you are covered. In most states it is illegal to operate a motor vehicle without insurance.

Disability Insurance:

- This insurance allows for a person to pay bills when there is a disability (illness or accident). If your husband has passed you may want to explore this option rather than be a burden to your children or other family members in the future.

FUNERAL EXPENSES

Planning for a funeral can be a daunting project. However, it is easiest to think in stages and once the task is broken down into manageable steps, you will find the process does not have to stressful. I have listed important steps for you to consider:
- There are two forms of body disposition - Burial (either in the ground or in a mausoleum - above the ground) or cremation (burning of the body and ashes scattered or placed in an urn.).
- You can donate the body to science. However after the institution is finished, the body is given back to the family for burial.
- A permanent place to visit after the death is important to many people. If you choose cremation, you may want to consider burying the ashes. If scattered, save a small amount as a keepsake and either put in an urn or substitute another form of remembrance either in your home or on the grounds.
- You must secure a burial plot prior to the actual funeral. Visit local cemeteries to compare options and prices. Buy what you

can afford.   Additionally, I would recommend you consider a cemetery close to your home and one that is accessible.   Often we want our loved ones to be buried in their hometown which can be several hundred miles away.   Then you do not have an opportunity to visit and make sure the site is well attended.

- Funeral homes often have a list of goods and services that describe in detail what you need to know to make a prudent decision.   You will need to think about the casket, burial vault, and the clothing in which your spouse will be interred.
- Choosing a casket is a matter of personal choice and affordability.   You can buy a casket for under $1,000 or as much as $10,000 or more.
  Caskets are made from metal or wood, with several varieties in each category.   More distinctive looks now include lifestyle caskets personally reflecting the deceased's life.
- The casket is placed inside the burial vault at the cemetery for the entombment.   Caskets will deteriorate with age and the vault prevents this from happening.   Vaults can be a simple concrete liner or a sealed vault.   If you are using a mausoleum, a vault is not necessary.
- The clothing can be purchased either from the funeral home or you can bring in items from the closet.   My personal preference was to put my husband in something comfortable from home.   If your spouse hated suits, do not feel you must make him go through eternity in one!
- There are other considerations such as flowers for the ceremony, a listing in the local newspaper, a donation to the local church, temple or synagogue hosting the services, and a wake or reception after the funeral that will have to be dealt with.
- You may need to provide the funeral home with the deceased's birth certificate, marriage license, legal name, home address and phone number, occupation, employer (with address), veteran's status with serial number, parent's and sibling's names, spouse's name (maiden, also), children's names and religious affiliation.
- Permanent memorials mark the location at the cemetery of your loved one.   They can be a simple marker or a grand tribute depending again on your personal preference.   Consult with the cemetery to learn their guidelines before making any permanent decisions.   Since it will take some time to get the final product, you can think of this after the funeral.
- The final services can be formal, informal, and religious or not.

- Traditional tributes are the most common. The body is viewed at a funeral home, the services are religious, and the body is then taken with the followers to the cemetery. If the body is to be cremated, it is taken to the crematory either prior to or after the service.
- A personalized service usually takes place at the funeral home. A short tribute from family and friends takes place with celebratory items and pictures used in the proceedings.
- Whichever you choose, make sure you consider the wishes of the deceased, make sure you have a time line in mind (length of service, etc.) and have an actual schedule of events to keep your pace intact.
- List a charity or organization to which you wish any donations to be forwarded. Most people send a floral tribute. While nice, these are limited in longevity. A donation is always a wonderful way to remember a loved one.

SOCIAL SECURITY

When a spouse dies you can collect social security if:
- You are a widow or widower, 60 years or older, or 50 years or older and disabled.
- You are a widow who is caring for a child under the age of sixteen, or a disabled child receiving Social Security benefits. Benefits will remain for your children, even if you remarry, as long as they are under sixteen years of age, or disabled and entitled to benefits.
- If your spouse had enough credits, a special one-time payment of $255.00 will be made to the widow.
- *You must apply for benefits...* no one notifies you and they are not paid automatically.
- You can apply for Medicare benefits at age 65. Plan on making application at least three months prior to your birthday.
- You may need the following documents: death certificate, birth certificate of the deceased, Social Security card of the deceased, a copy of the marriage certificate, birth certificate of the applicant and any minor children, disability proof for children over 18, and a receipt for the funeral.
- Widow's benefits will be from 71 ½ percent of your husband's benefit amount if you take that at age 60 to 100 percent at age 65

or 66 depending the current regulations in place. You are also allowed to use your work benefits to apply for Social Security at age 62 and then receive your full widow's benefits at age 65 or 66. Also, if you plan on delaying retirement until age 70 your benefits increase 6 percent each year from 65 to 70.

- If you remarry you are still entitled to receive benefits under your deceased husband's record. However, you cannot receive widow's benefits and additional benefits from your new husband. There are so many options available that you must talk with a Social Security Administration representative. Once again it will be necessary to fill out papers, and provide an original death certificate. You can usually talk to a representative by phone that will mail you all the papers and process your claim. You can reach the agency at 1-800-772-1213 or 1-800-234-5772 or visit the website at www.ssa.gov.

VETERAN'S BENEFITS

- The family of an honorably discharged military veteran may be entitled to a number of benefits. As with Social Security, the benefits must be applied for and are not automatic. For veteran benefit claims you will need: a death certificate, veteran's discharge papers, copy of the marriage certificate, birth certificates of veteran's minor children and an itemized receipt of the veteran's funeral bill.
- Contact your local or regional office of the US. Department of Veteran's Affairs for information on benefits and claims procedures. The national offices is 1-202-872-1151 or write to Department of Veteran Affairs, 810 Vermont Avenue, NW, Washington D.C. 20420

FINANCIAL FORECAST

Intelligent investing in your future is a must. No matter how large or small the amount, the savings will be the cornerstone of your financial future. Now that you are the sole provider for your security, consider the following suggestions:

- Investments grow with time. There are tested principles that help reduce risk and allow your investments to grow. Do not be impatient or expect to make a fast fortune.

- Assess your tolerance for risk. If you are near retirement age, your investments should be less volatile than if you are in your thirties or early forties and able to take more financial risk.
- Invest regularly. Put a set amount away every month. If you have a 401K, put in the maximum amount, if possible.
- The government is now helping investors by making several retirement accounts available, which are tax deferred.
- Save early for large ticket items. If you will have a child going to college or need to purchase a home or automobile, now is the time to start saving.
- Remember to diversify. You need to have your money allocated in different types of securities... also called asset allocation. This method reduces risk and improves your total return.

Investment Options:
- Cash equivalents - money market funds, CD's, treasury bills. They are a short-term investment and offer a low rate of return.
- Bonds pay a fixed interest on a regular basis. Municipalities, the federal government and corporations issue bonds. Bonds provide a steady income and are tax-free but do not protect against inflation.
- With stocks, you become a shareholder in a corporation. You are betting that the companies are going to prosper, succeed and make money for your portfolio. Stock prices fluctuate based on the company's stock on any given day. Any negative information about the company can result in a lower stock price. However, it is important to remember that when you invest in the stock market, *it is for long-term gains.* Over time, stocks have always risen and provide the best hedge against inflation.
- Mutual Funds pool your money, with other investors, to purchase a larger portfolio. You can get investment advice to help you with your personal objective in mind.

There are also tax-deferred plans available that you should be cognizant of:

- IRA's are individual retirement accounts to save for your future. These allow your dollars to grow on a tax-deferred basis. New laws enable you to contribute more than before, especially if you are over 50. There is also a ROTH IRA, which allows the investor to pay taxes in advance of using the IRA at age 59 ½. Check with a financial consultant to make the best choice for your personal needs.

- 401K plans are able to invest pretax dollars to an account through your employer. You make the investment choices and many times the employer matches your contributions up to a pre-set limit.
- Annuities invest in tax-deferred annuities to build your retirement assets. Your investment comes back in periodic annuity payments. Earnings on your assets grow tax-deferred and this method can offer you a powerful retirement tool.
- Pension plans are a retirement tool for you or your spouse. Check with his employer to learn what you need to know about the distribution. Often, you must wait until your spouse would have been eligible to retire before receiving benefits, but many companies also offer a buy-out, which can then be invested in other areas.

This is an overview of financial planning to help you understand things a little better. But, please, talk to an accountant or a financial planner who can help you set up your appropriate needs.

ESTATE PLANNING

Whether or not your husband was astute enough to make estate plans, make sure that your estate plans are well thought out and up-to-date. The government could end up with nearly everything you own. There are new federal laws which allow your heirs to inherit dollars with no penalties, but this does not save them from state inheritance taxes or death tax. There are also legal fees, probate costs, and other expenses.

Some things to be aware of:

- Make sure you have joint tenancy or ownership, or tenancy by the entirety with survivor's right (two names on the deed) of your house. This insures that if your husband should die, your house passes directly on to you, bypassing probate. Property passes to the survivor within weeks rather than six months or more in probate.
- You can also use joint tenancy with rights of survivorship for bank, brokerage and savings and loan accounts. It alleviates the

assets being frozen and allows you to withdraw funds up to one half of the amount of the account. This process can also be used for automobiles.

- Upon a death, if you have a safe deposit box (which is a good way to keep your valuables) the state may come in and seal the box until an audit can be done for inheritance tax purposes. If you have joint tenancy, you may want to keep your personal belongings separate in the box so that proof of ownership upon your spouse's death can be verified. The remaining estate can then be removed for tax purposes and your personal property will be available to you.

- If you sell your principal residence after a death, there may still be capital gains due if another home is not purchased. Your husband's exclusion ($250,000 single, $500,000 a couple) can still be claimed but may only be used the year of the death (if not previously used). Your home must be your primary residence for two years to qualify for the full exclusion.

- Make sure your will specifies exactly what is to be given away and to whom. Often a will is so vague that battles ensue because children or grandchildren may want the same heirloom and it is not spelled out in the will who will get the piece. Be specific with each item you own.

- Estates pass first to a spouse and then to heirs. However, with no will in place the surviving spouse gets $50,000 with further distributions to come from any excess. Next in line are the children (including legally adopted) and then the parents of the deceased followed by siblings and other remote relatives of the deceased. There are printed general guidelines as to how the court divides an estate when there is no will. You can by-pass all this red tape and ensure estate matters are handled the way you, or your spouse, want. The most important thing to remember is: MAKE A WILL. There is simply no excuse not to have this done in advance. It will save a great deal of heartache and stress for the survivors. Make sure it is executed, signed, reviewed annually, and any old copies destroyed.

- A living will serves as your decision document in the matters of health care. It is designed to direct family, doctors, hospitals, and others what to do in life sustaining circumstances. Your last wishes and general guidelines will be met.

- You have a lifetime exemption of $675,000 (this will gradually increase to $1 million in the year 2006) to give away to your heirs during your life or to leave at your death. You can give your property (value unlimited) to your spouse free of federal estate tax. Be aware that as the remaining spouse you may have all the assets transferred to you and your heirs will be faced with the tax burden after your passing. Consult a financial planner to make provisions for that event.

- Taxes are due nine months after the date of death. Be sure to consult with an attorney about local estate laws. If you cannot afford an attorney, call the Legal Aid organization in your town. They can make some recommendations.
- You can give $11,000 a year to any one without incurring federal gift tax. You can also make charitable bequests, all of which are tax deductible.
- If your husband has amassed a fortune, it is wise to investigate family trusts, which preserve assets for later distribution.
- Life insurance trusts can build up additional assets to be used at your death and are not subject to federal estate tax.
- Make sure if there is a second marriage, there is a prenuptial agreement to protect your assets so that they can provide for the future of children from the first marriage.

Consult an accountant for tax matters, an attorney for estate planning, and a financial planner for investing. Have the team communicate with each other and agree on the best plan for you. Using multiple advisors also builds in a checks and balance system for your peace of mind.

Pat Nowak

Finale

After death, there is never a finale. Not a day goes by that a thought, word or action reminds me of Cas. It can be a favorite song, a comment from a friend or a glimpse of my grandson in a certain light, and that moment can still bring melancholy moments. After all, he was supposed to be the one to walk my daughter down the aisle, pace the floors with me when my grandchildren were born and finally, retired, was going to make me tired old bologna sandwiches or winter in Marco Island. Florida, while I toiled in Ohio. Of course, that will never be.

It is never easy loosing a soul mate. The initial loneliness and solitude were daunting for me. I was used to continuous social activity and going in several directions. I learned that to be a survivor, it was necessary to take the time to find out who I really was and what I needed in my life for my personal happiness. My husband was a fisherman; I hated fishing so I took golf and tennis lessons. I enrolled in art and pottery classes and volunteered more. The sense of pride I felt as I accomplished one more thing was most gratifying. It became easier to make new plans and dream. This book came about because I embarked on a freelance career, as a Lifestyle columnist, for a local paper. My weekly column proved to be the impetus to get me going on the book. A year later the book is finished...now I can think of other books that need to be written. None of this would have been possible, without dreaming.

The death and fire have taught me a valuable lesson...change is needed to prune away dead wood, so that your roots receive the strength to grow deep and strong, and though the pruning may be too harsh at times, we emerge more productive, patient and wiser.

I waited to enter the dating game. I thought it was necessary, for me, to learn to live alone. I was also fortunate to have a career that allowed me access to several social events yearly, and I did not need a date to attend. Dating can be tough for someone who has been married to the same man for twenty-seven years and I probably wouldn't have gone on the first one if it hadn't been for a friend who insisted. I learned that in dating, the first relationship is usually transitional.

121

Just as you are spreading your wings in your new life, you realize what works and doesn't in a relationship. For me, it was my career. A woman who has visual notoriety in a community frightens many men. The most important thing I learned from the "dating game" is that I have to be me and if I had to change to sustain a relationship, then the connection is doomed from the beginning. A good balance of give and take is necessary for success. I am still not married...but have discovered that a relationship succeeds when there is a level of comfort for both parties.

My children have both married the partners that went through the dark days with us. My son Marty, a counselor needed more time for his grief process. A chance encounter, with a patient in a hospital, he worked for seemed to put his mind at rest. Through him, he realized that his father truly loved and appreciated him. His new wife, Heather, a marketing representative for a bank, is the perfect partner for him. After dating for ten years, I believe Cas would be pleased.

My daughter Laura, a stay-at-home mother of two, Liam Casimir and Rae Isabella is enjoying the hectic camaraderie of being a mother, mentor, chauffeur, cook, nurse etc. Her husband Douglas is a construction supervisor. He is finishing his degree in engineering and is a wonderful father.

Both children honor their father in so many ways and I see some of Cas's traits in both. Though the death was difficult for each of them, in different ways, they have not let the death destroy their lives. I am so proud of them and try to tell them, often, how much they mean to me, even when the male contingent is in the "tease mom" mode.

As for my grandchildren...they breathe new life into me. Their childlike exploration is a delight. Every Saturday, Liam and I have an adventure...it can be nothing more than going to the grocery store. The fun we have is priceless.

I calculate that in a couple years he will be too old and then it will be Rae's turn. After that, I can have a succession of Saturday adventures until I'm at least seventy or older.

We still get together often, take vacations as a family and remember their father fondly. I would like to leave you one thought...from a card I saved, written by Amanda Bradley:

Those we love are never really lost to us; we feel them in so many special ways....
Through friends they always cared about and dreams they left behind,
In beauty that they added to our days...in words of wisdom we still carry with us
And memories that will never be gone...those we love are never really lost to us...
For everywhere their special love lives on.

Please allow peace and serenity to enter your life...gather strength from the earth around you. Pick up the sand and make sandcastles. Your new life is up to you to build or destroy. You have the free will, to pursue your vision of freedom and spiritual awakening. Make it a wonderful journey!

ABOUT THE AUTHOR

Biography............Pat Nowak, The ABC's of Widowhood

Pat Nowak is a Toledo native, one of the four daughters of Robert and Hedwig Stack.

Her career as a fashion director for two local department chains, the owner of a Public Relations firm and her subsequent position at Seaway Food Town Supermarkets have allowed her access to the highly visible world of broadcast and print media. She has been a media spokesperson for over twenty years, directed and co-hosted a highly visible morning radio talk show, written, produced and appeared in company advertising and for televised preview shows.

Her journalism career began out of necessity. Suddenly, as new widow, fluent in writing press materials and a Lifestyles column, she searched for something readable that could help her grieving soul. Finding great stories about personal triumph helped but there was little that addressed precisely and with clarity what every new widow faces. Thus _The ABC's of Widowhood_ came about, the help all women over the age of forty (widowed or not) need to get their emotional and financial worlds in balance. The book celebrates the spirit of hope and allows a woman to discover the path to being reborn through perseverance, courage and determination.

Pat's family includes son Martin (Heather), daughter Laura Nowak-Glover (Douglas) and grandchildren Liam Casimir and Rae Isabella. She resides in Holland, Ohio.

Printed in the United States
17822LVS00002B/178-273